VALLEY OF THE CRAFTSMEN

VALLEY OF THE CRAFTSMEN

A Pictorial History

Scottish Rite Freemasonry
in America's Southern Jurisdiction
1801-2001

EDITOR
William L. Fox

ART DIRECTION, DESIGN AND
PROJECT MANAGEMENT
Frank Glickman and Matthew Monk
Frank Glickman, Inc.

WRITING
Henry Scammell

CONSULTING HISTORIAN
Arturo de Hoyos

ARCHIVAL RESEARCH
Mark Fastoso

PRODUCTION COORDINATION
Susan McNally

COPY EDITING
Catherine Dexter Martin

PRINTING AND BINDING
Eurografica SPA, Vicenza, Italy

For a complete list of picture credits, see page 265,
an extension of the copyright page.

Printed and bound in Italy

Published 2001 by The Supreme Council, 33°,
to commemorate its 200th anniversary.

Library of Congress Control Number: 2001087582

ISBN: 0-9708749-1-X

CONTENTS

" And as for the villages, with their fields, some of the people
of Judah lived in Kiriatharba.... The people of Benjamin also lived
from Geba onward...Lod, and Ono, the valley of the craftsmen."

– Nehemiah 11:25-35

This pictorial narrative considers a mere two centuries, but its title is drawn from a more distant reference point, going back at least twenty-five centuries. Without invoking the historian's version of the relativity theory, the simple fact is that the Scottish Rite of Freemasonry, one of the premier international fraternal orders of the 19th and 20th centuries, lived in two eras at once—in the ancient world it tried to recover and the modern one it tried to improve.

Like many organizations with a time-honored history, the Scottish Rite documents its past in the tangibility of faces, official papers, portraits, material objects, and buildings. Expressed algebraically, history is the evidence of people added to places divided by time, a formula consciously present here. And yet, the Scottish Rite may be unique among community institutions, because it also traces its symbolic roots into worlds that perhaps never were or, if they were, to moments better defined as philosophical reveries somehow apprehended by historical imagination. This second kind of impression is the source of the book's title, expressing a timeless accord that Freemasons affirm with all builders and repairers in every generation.

The major historical works in the Hebrew Bible, scanning the promise and tribulation of national life between Joshua and Job, might easily have concluded at the lowest point in the generations-old story with the fall of Jerusalem. The destruction of King Solomon's temple was arguably the worst hour in a thousand-year history. It was a completely devastating moment, though it would not be the last time the beautiful city succumbed to ruin. Instead, the extraordinary epic of a people's rise, decline, and exile concludes in a dramatic return of the captives facing the daunting possibilities of restoration. The final installment of the epic saga is told through the perspective of the heroic leader Nehemiah, whose sole purpose was to rebuild and reoccupy Jerusalem.

In Nehemiah's memoir, the immediate challenge was to repair the walls of Jerusalem, inspire the returning people's will to do so, and address all sorts of internal dissent combined with external adversity. Restoring the holy city was a moral imperative. In the end, the initiative succeeded and Jerusalem was once again inhabited, but in a most curious way. Nehemiah completed his account of rehabilitating the fallen city with a census report. He described an arrangement that required each village to send one out of ten citizens to live in Jerusalem. He enumerated the participating towns, and characterized one of the places sending its quota to Jerusalem as "the valley of the craftsmen."

When the Scottish Rite of Freemasonry came into official existence in 1801 with the formation of the Supreme Council, the leaders turned to the ancient east and west for their inspiration. They remembered Jerusalem and Athens, one symbolizing the measures of beauty from the east, the other the classical order from the west. The evolving higher degree system of Freemasonry, long since an attractive ritual tradition among European nations and their colonies, envisioned common meanings induced by dual sources of civilization. They were drawing from the wisdom traditions of the Orient and the Occident that sought order from chaos in the development of a moral life.

Freemasons often refer to their fraternity as *the Craft*. It is a term of pride that, like quality workmanship itself, implies the premium standard of its own guild or trade. There is, in addition, a second symbolic meaning in the title of this book. The Scottish Rite, after its first half-century, organized itself by *Orients*, corresponding in the United States to individual states or territories, and within these jurisdictions the cities were named *Valleys*, forming local consociations of Scottish Rite lodges. Thus, "the valley of the craftsmen" captures exactly the proper fraternal designation of the places and people who have represented Scottish Rite Freemasons in local and historical contexts.

Resembling the ancient builders of the second Jerusalem drawn from a surrounding landscape of settlements and communities, the builders and preservers of the Scottish Rite dwelled in their own equivalent valleys of craftsmen for two centuries. It is our hope that the reader of this book will somehow discover a fresh vista of American history, something like the surprise of a wayside overlook along the mountain rim. In the transaction between eye and imagination, it is also reasonable to expect that within these pages, the people to be met, the buildings visited, and the scenes observed would come alive in "the valley of the craftsmen." In that valley, a firm, warm handshake of fellowship has gripped thousands of men, extending across the years to a day of jubilee in 2001.

— W L F

The project was conceived almost immediately after the publication of the history of the Southern (and founding) Jurisdiction of the Scottish Rite that I authored a few years ago, *Lodge of the Double-Headed Eagle.* The idea for the pictorial history as one centerpiece of the bicentennial observance originated when the Supreme Council member for South Carolina, H. Wallace Reid, called me in Washington with his idea for a very ambitious anniversary program in 2001.

With no more than an encouraging word, Wallace Reid was quickly on his way to Washington to meet with Grand Commander C. Fred Kleinknecht and Executive Director W. Gene Sizemore. In less than an hour, he made his case, and in that instant I was invited to plan, direct, and edit a pictorial history that would represent, in the words of Fred Kleinknecht, "nothing but first-class quality."

All well and good, but the fact remained, I had no experience whatsoever in the enterprise of a museum-quality photographic retrospective. I was entering an unknown valley of specialized craftsmanship.

To get started, Gene Sizemore and I made several planning excursions to Charleston, South Carolina, always guided around the city and low country by the knowledgeable Wallace Reid. These trips stirred my imagination, a crucially necessary exercise that required me to shift from thinking about history in words to seeing history in pictures. Visiting historic churches and synagogues, inspecting hallowed Christian and Jewish burying grounds, walking the Battery and narrow streets, and handling rare Masonic artifacts all contributed to the pictures that were forming in my head for this book.

The next step was to put together a team of experts. I turned to the Office of the President at The George Washington University for advice because I particularly admired a pictorial history the university published on the occasion of its 175th anniversary. President Stephen Joel Trachtenberg recommended (*summa cum laude*) Frank Glickman of Boston as among the best book designers in the country. I called, and to my relief, Frank was available. Out of this collaboration has emerged a cherished friendship for both of us. Together with his gifted associate, Matthew Monk, Frank was able to translate ideas into form through exquisite craftsmanship seen on every single page.

3

The endeavor required other talents that neither Frank nor I could supply alone. Mark Fastoso was involved in several projects at the Washington public television station WETA, but readily came on board to be the book's photo researcher. His eye and doggedness made all the difference in accumulating visual material for the book now in hand.

Henry Scammell is a professional writer with book and magazine credits of remarkable dimensions from aviation history to medical research. This assignment called for an individual with a wide breadth of general knowledge and a deep sensitivity to the complex nature of fraternal orders in American society. Henry's varieties of experience, penetrating insights, and reliable wit provided the project the instructive verbal framing around the pictures.

While I have "done" plenty of history as a teacher and writer, it was imperative that the venture enlist a consulting historian. Arturo de Hoyos is a Masonic historian of immense passion for his subject, the perfect special advisor for this project. In checking facts, assisting in the search for material and selection of images, and serving as a resource to all of us, Art was a vital presence in many aspects of the undertaking.

As talented colleagues bringing the added value of wisdom to numerous critical junctures, Frank Glickman, Mark Fastoso, Henry Scammell, and Arturo de Hoyos put me in a somewhat negative accounting position as the book evolved. I trust, however, that my fervor, admiration, and gratitude were sufficient in the end to balance the ledger.

Gene Sizemore continues to prove that running a tight ship can be done in the calmest manner. I could not imagine a steadier hand than Gene's to guide the Scottish Rite's bicentennial hopes into its triumphant culmination, of which this pictorial history is but one part of a grand moment.

Finally, Fred Kleinknecht did so much more than simply endorse the concept of a pictorial history. His *laissez faire* demeanor toward the creation of this book was, for us, the highest measure of support. From the beginning, his first principles were manifest, chief of which is his ultimate belief in people, especially those who have earnestly put their hands to a demanding task. His confidence in me personally was a constant source of reassurance. For that and for his friendship, I am thankful.

William L. Fox

BETWEEN THE American Revolution and the end of the twentieth century stand only two men, known to each other…connected through a common association with the Scottish Rite, Southern Jurisdiction. C. Fred Kleinknecht, elected Grand Commander in 1985, was hired to work at the Supreme Council by John Henry Cowles in the 1940s; as a young man, Cowles met Albert Pike, who once passed an afternoon with him in the older man's library. Going back another sixty years or so, Albert Pike, as a fifteen-year-old boy, shook hands with Lafayette sometime in 1824. Lafayette was, of course, instrumental in the success of George Washington's army.

From *Lodge of the Double-Headed Eagle: Two Centuries of Scottish Rite Freemasonry in America's Southern Jurisdiction* by William L. Fox

The Banner of the Scottish Rite, carried to the moon by astronaut Edwin "Buzz" Aldrin on Apollo 11, represents a rich tradition of leadership, brotherhood, and commitment which began before the founding of America. Almost incredibly, the astronaut who carried this emblem into space was directly connected, through an unbroken chain of only five handshakes, with the Father of Our Country. Many of the same visionaries and patriots who laid the cornerstone for the fledgling nation also played a role in the birth of the American fraternity. Their successors would extend their vision to embrace the world. This pictorial history, which celebrates the first two centuries of the Scottish Rite, Southern Jurisdiction, traces the epochal linkage symbolized by those handshakes.

1717–1801

FORGING THE FRATERNAL CHAIN

From Washington to Lafayette

10

THE OLDEST FRATERNITY in the United States, Freemasonry has been famously described as "a system of morality veiled in allegory and illustrated by symbols." Well established in the American colonies for at least two decades before the War of Independence, Freemasonry traces its formal ancestry back to the Grand Lodge of England and to the first meeting of four London lodges at the Apple Tree Tavern in 1716. Less formally, its lineage dates back another century to the Lodge of Edinburgh in 1600.

The origins of Freemasonry's quest for philosophy and wisdom traditionally lie in antiquity, with ancient Egypt, Greece, Israel, and Rome. ☞ Historian David Stevenson places the starting point of the modern institution in the English "documents known as the 'Old Charges' or 'Old Constitutions.' Like other medieval trades, the masons had their craft organizations or guilds, and their mythical histories stressing antiquity and the importance of the crafts, closely linking them with religious and moral concepts." ☞ One of the purposes of a guild was to preserve and pass on the mysteries of the craft. Over time, those mysteries expanded to include intellectual and ethical standards far beyond the simple secrets of the trade. The craft of masonry, with its emphasis on geometry and claims to spiritual descent from builders of the monuments of antiquity, became a brotherhood of rich symbolism and ritual. Its appeal grew with its membership, extending to distinguished men of all callings: scholars, aristocrats, merchants, actors, soldiers, statesmen. Those whose relationship to the guilds or lodges was intellectual and spiritual rather than specifically based on the craft of stonecutting were granted honorary memberships, hence the term Accepted Mason. The concept proved so popular that eventually the Accepted member-ship far outnumbered the practitioners of the trade. Meetings utilized the sym-bolism of stonecraft to create allegory in the ritual of an eclectic and vastly expanded brotherhood. By the second half of the eighteenth century, Freemasonry was the leading social institution, after churches, in both Europe and North America. Its membership enjoyed representation in politics, commerce, and influential philosophical circles. As the American colonies began their difficult, painful, and visionary evolution into nationhood, Freemasons on both sides of the ocean and on both sides of the issue stood in the forefront—as powerful defenders of the status quo, and as movers and shapers of the world to come.

George Washington and
the Marquis de Lafayette
were as closely bound
in the fraternity of
Freemasonry as in their
common quest for the
independence of the new
United States.

16

Masonic constitution, 1723. The Reverend James D. Anderson compiled the "Old Charges" (ancient regulations governing Freemasons) and published the first sanctioned *Constitutions of the Free-Masons* in 1723. They remain the basis of Masonic law to this day.

Both the operative and speculative qualities of Freemasonry are embodied in this Limoges enamel image, probably of an eighteenth-century Fellowcraft. In his right hand he holds a trowel, and in his left a "tracing board" or symbolic architectural design. The apron is turned up and buttoned to his vest to protect his clothes, prefiguring the modern "bib" or flap on the speculative Freemason's apron.

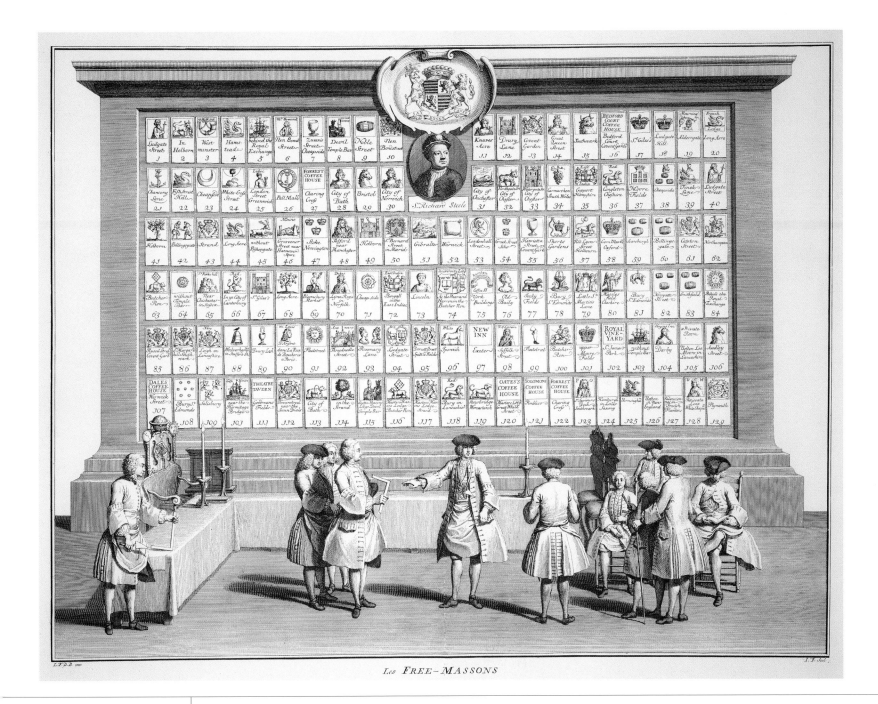

An idealized Masonic
ceremony takes place
in front of a 1735 lodge
register in London. In
the listing of recognized
Masonic lodges, Number
126 is "Boston in New
England."

The Ceremony of Making a Free-Mason.

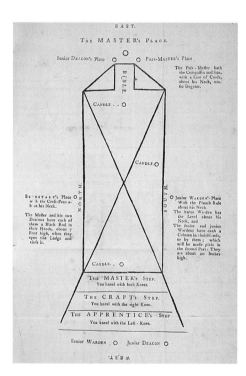

18

Masonic initiation ceremony, London, 1766. The Worshipful Master is seated at the head of a rectangular table, a position traditionally termed "the East." During the initiation, the candidate is led around the table to various officers. The design of modern Masonic lodge rooms is based on the shape of these early tables.

An English lodge plan of the same period, drawn on the floor of the meeting hall.

A mock procession of Freemasons is led by a monkey dressed in Masonic white gloves and apron in *The Mystery of Masonry brought to Light by ye Gormogons,* by English satirist and Freemason William Hogarth.

A debauched and wounded Worshipful Master and his servant stumble home from a session of Masonic revelry in *Night* (1738), by William Hogarth. Prior to the erection of dedicated rooms, the "lodge" was not so much a place as an event held in private residences or taverns such as those lining this street in Charing Cross. Masons would make a

chalk or charcoal drawing of King Solomon's Temple and other symbolic images on a table or the floor and hold their rituals around it. This engraving appeared the same year as the Reverend James D. Anderson's second edition of his *Masonic Constitutions.*

Invented, Painted, Engraved & Publifhed by Wm. Hogarth March 25, 1738, according to Act of Parliamt.

NIGHT

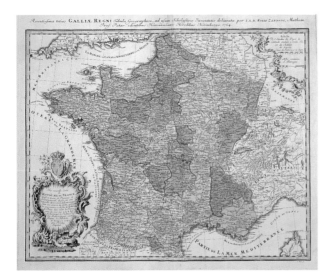

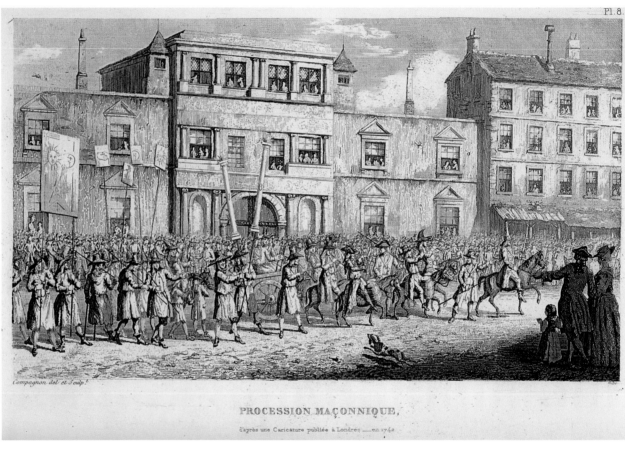

PROCESSION MAÇONNIQUE,

d'après une Caricature publiée à Londres ___ en 1742.

20 Despite its name, the origins of the Scottish Rite lie in France, not Britain. Living in exile in Bordeaux, a Scottish Jacobite named Andrew Michael Ramsay (1686–1743) is believed to have invented a Masonic mythology based on the medieval Knights of St. John of Jerusalem. At almost the same time, a French political exile, Jean Theophile Desaguliers, a Huguenot, sought asylum in Britain. He helped reshape the London Grand Lodge to the deist tenets of the Enlightenment.

One of the earliest known Masons in the colonies was John Skew, who entered the brotherhood in Aberdeen, Scotland, in 1682, shortly before moving to New Jersey. By 1775, the movement was truly international, with Grand Lodges in France, England, Germany, Holland, Italy, Poland, Scotland, Spain, Sweden, and Switzerland.

Clavel's *Procession Maçonnique* depicts an authentic English Masonic parade, circa 1742. Leading this procession is the tyler, or guardian, wearing an unusual hat and carrying a flaming sword. On the far left two Masons hold a tracing board, or lodge plan, with the working tools of Freemasonry and the sun and moon.

Master satirist Voltaire (pseudonym of François Marie Arouet) was Benjamin Franklin's personal friend and fellow member of the Lodge of the Nine Muses in Paris.

Voltaire's Masonic apron.

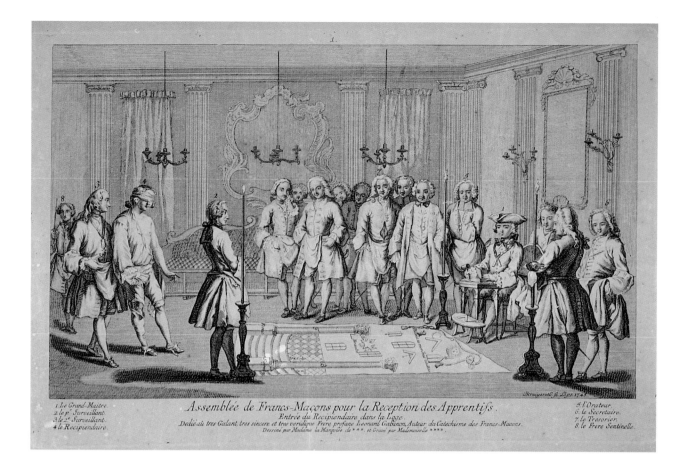

Illustrations from the eighteenth-century *Catechism of French Masonry.*

Assembly for Reception of Apprentices depicts the roles of the Grand Master, Senior Warden, Junior Warden, the person to be initiated, Orator, Secretary, Treasurer, and Tyler.

The initiated apprentice swears never to reveal the Masonic mysteries.

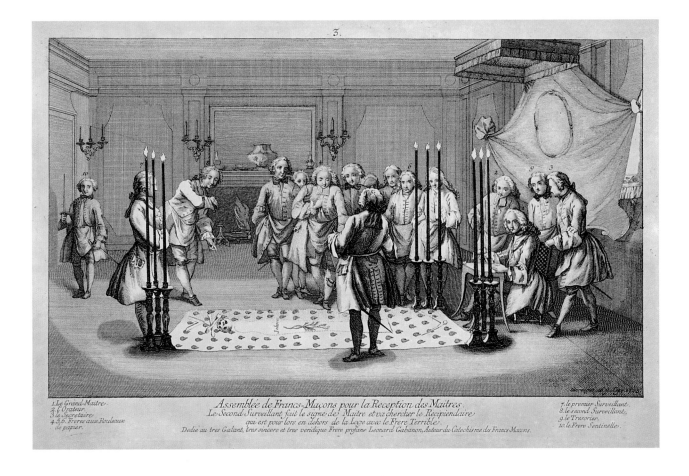

Assembly for Reception of the Masters changes the order of participants and introduces the Brothers of the Scrolls. The Junior Warden is shown bowing at his entrance to the lodge, prior to making the sign of a Master Mason.

The Master's ceremony continues with the entrance of the initiate into the lodge, on the point of a sword.

Assemblée de Francs-Maçons pour la Reception des Maitres.
On couche le Recipiendaire sur le Cercueil dessiné dans la Loge.

Dedié au très Galant, tres sincere et tres veridique Frere profane Leonard Gabanon, Auteur du Catechisme des Francs-Maçons.

1. Le Grand Maitre.
2. le p.ᵉ Surveillant.
3. le 2.ᵉ Surveillant.
4. Recipiendaire que l'on couche sur le Cercueil.

5.6.7. Recipiendaires a qui le Grand Maitre n'a pas encore donné l'accolade.
8. l'Orateur.
9. le Secretaire.
10. le Tresorier.
11. le Frere Sentinelle.

Representing the slain architect of King Solomon's Temple, the initiated Master Mason is supported by his fellow Masons while being lowered into a symbolic grave.

Symbolically "buried"
by a shroud, the initiate's
location is pointed out
by the tips of the mem-
bers' swords as the
Grand Master prepares
to "raise" him.

The Master's initiation
ceremony ends with the
Grand Master "raising"
the candidate by embrac-
ing him on the "points
of fellowship," after which
he is told the secret Word
of a Master Mason.

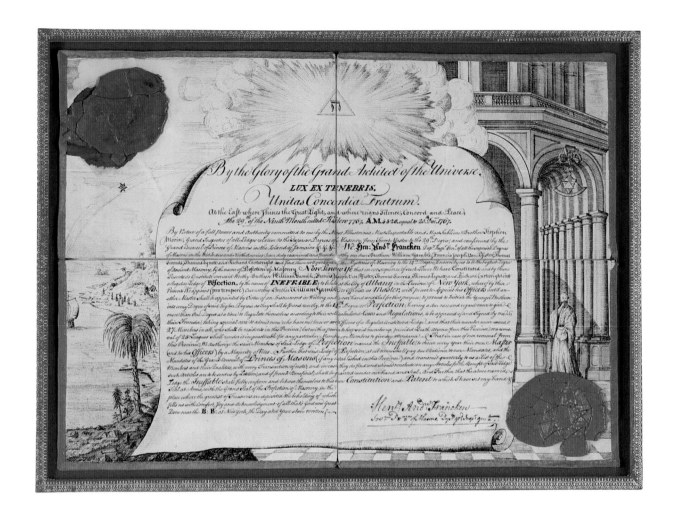

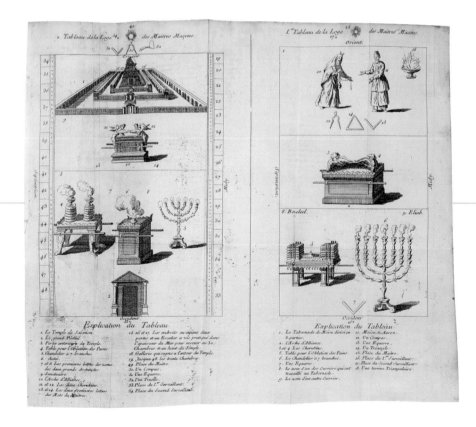

Pages from *Le Parfait Maçon* (1744) depict the tools and ritual of eighteenth-century French Freemasonry. This was the first printed source to describe rituals which would become part of the Scottish Rite.

Patent of the Ineffable and Sublime Grand Lodge of Perfection, Albany, New York, issued by Henry A. Francken, December 20, 1767. The following June, for the first time in the American colonies, degrees of the Rite of Perfection were presented at that lodge—another major step in the evolution of the Scottish Rite.

FROM WASHINGTON TO LAFAYETTE

A young French noble-
man, the Marquis de
Lafayette probably
became a Mason at the
age of eighteen in 1775,
a period when the appeal
of the movement was
growing among the
social elite.

This badge, again depict-
ing Lafayette in his
Continental Army gener-
al's uniform, is from the
dinner given in his honor
by the Grand Lodge,
Washington Hall, New
York, on September 20,
1824.

On this same return
visit to the new nation
Lafayette met a gifted
student, poet, and violin-
ist from Newburyport,
Massachusetts, fifteen-
year-old Albert Pike.

Lafayette wore this
Masonic apron at
the Washington Hall
reception.

Masonic apron cases, decorated with fine beadwork, from the late eighteenth and early nineteenth centuries.

This French Masonic apron, circa 1800, incorporates many of the symbols found on tracing boards. The skull and crossbones are emblems of mortality; the sprig of evergreen symbolizes the hope of a future life; the whole is surrounded by the uroboros, an emblem of eternity.

Masonic encyclopedist Albert G. Mackey defines a summons as a "warning to appear at the meeting of a Lodge or other Masonic body." This 1811 example from Philadelphia follows the pattern of a lodge summons printed for the "Antient" York Masons of Halifax in 1784, its design based on early tracing boards.

Silver medallion depicting symbols from a lodge summons.

THE
CONSTITUTIONS
OF THE
FREE-MASONS.

CONTAINING THE

History, Charges, Regulations, &c.
of that moſt Ancient and Right
Worſhipful FRATERNITY.

For the Uſe of the LODGES.

LONDON Printed; *Anno* 5723.
Re-printed in *Philadelphia* by ſpecial Order, for the Uſe
of the Brethren in NORTH-AMERICA.
In the Year of Maſonry 5734, *Anno Domini* 1734.

The American edition of James Anderson's *Constitutions of the Free-Masons* (1723) was printed by Benjamin Franklin in Philadelphia in 1734—the first Masonic publication in colonial America. (Franklin's picture is not a part of the book.)

This early tracing board (facing page, top) of Western Star Lodge No. 5, New York, includes the symbols of the three craft degrees, divided by levels. On either side of the structure are the rough and perfect ashlars, or stones, representing the vulgar and refined states of humanity. The bottom portion represents the checkered ground-floor pavement of King Solomon's Temple, where tradition maintains Entered Apprentice Masons met for work; the twenty-four-inch gauge and common gavel, near the rough ashlar, are their tools. The square and compasses rest on the Holy Bible, the triad comprising Masonry's "Great Lights." The second floor represents the Middle Chamber of King Solomon's Temple, with the working tools of the Fellowcraft Mason. The letter G is for Geometry, the fifth subject of the seven liberal arts, and for some Freemasons symbolizes the term for Deity. The third floor, representing the sanctum sanctorum or Holy of Holies of King Solomon's Temple, is decorated with emblems of the Master Mason Degree to evoke the mortality of the human body. Above this, veiled from view, the "Celestial Lodge" is presided over by the All-Seeing Eye of God.

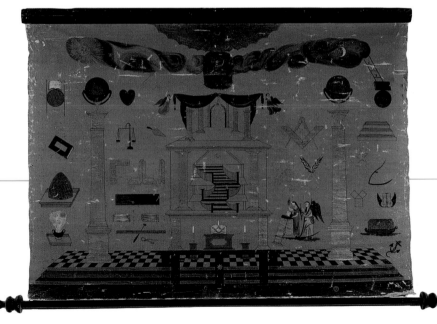

A tracing board from Cherry Valley, when that portion of upstate New York was still a part of the American frontier.

Another early tracing board, from Hobard, New York, retains the traditional symbols of the three degrees, although its arrangement is haphazard. Lacking the structure of an architectural motif, the three "symbolic supports"—the triple pillars of Wisdom, Strength, and Beauty—bear the craft's symbols. The Roman numerals on the bases label the pillars as the degrees of Entered Apprentice, Fellowcraft, and Master Mason.

Images of tracing boards and other Masonic symbols appear in a variety of utilitarian objects, such as these two pitchers and ceramic serving bowl. The frequent use of Masonic symbols on ordinary objects was a constant reminder to members of the fraternity that Freemasonry touched all aspects of their lives.

The first lodge of Freemasons in North America is believed to have been organized in Philadelphia's Old Tun Tavern in 1730–31.

These blown-molded flasks, popular throughout the early 1800s, bear traditional symbols of a Masonic tracing board.

Firing glasses have thick bottoms consistent with their role in Masonic banquets. Representing a cannon, they are "charged" with red or white wine which is drunk on the signal "fire," then brought down in unison sharply on the tabletop to simulate the report from a battery of artillery.

This symbolic rendering of a temple, executed while the Masonic movement was still entwined with tavern culture, prefigures the grand Masonic architecture of a future century.

Masonic symbolism appears in the door to this lantern, a type frequently displayed outside the homes, shops, and taverns of members in the seventeenth and eighteenth centuries and up through the early years of the Scottish Rite in America.

The Old Masonic Temple in Halifax, North Carolina, housed the Royal White Hart Lodge from January 14, 1771, to the start of the Revolution.

Worshipful Master's jewel from St. Andrew's Lodge, 1766.

Boston's Green Dragon Tavern was purchased by the Lodge of St. Andrew in 1764. Eleven years later, it was the site of General Joseph Warren's Masonic funeral.

The symbols on this
colonial American
powder horn identify its
owner as a Mason.

WASHINGTON AS A FREEMASON

G

AN ORDER WHOSE LEADING STAR IS PHILANTHROPY
LAFAYETTE

PAST GRAND MASTER OF THE GRAND LODGE OF TENNESSEE
JACKSON

CHARITY

HOPE

FAITH

BEAUTY

STRENGTH

WISDOM

BORN
Feb. 22.
A.D.1732

DIED
Dec. 14.
A.D.1799.

FORTITUDE   PRUDENCE

TEMPERANCE   JUSTICE

COMMANDER OF THE AMERICAN ARMY, 1775. PRESIDENT OF THE UNITED STATES, 1789.
INITIATED, NOVEMBER 4TH 1752, IN FREDERICKSBURG, LODGE No 4, VIRGINIA. PASSED, MARCH 3RD 1753 RAISED, AUGUST 4TH 1753.

Awake not his Slumbers, tread lightly around,
Tis the Grave of a Freeman, 'tis Liberty's mound,
Thy Name is immortal, our Freedom you won,
Brave Sire of Columbia, our own Washington.
Oh! wake not the Hero, his Battles are o'er,
Let him rest, calmly rest, on his dear native Shore,
While the Stars & the Stripes of our Country shall wave
O'er the Land that can boast of a Washington's Grave.

Disturb not his Slumbers, let Washington sleep,
'Neath the Boughs of the Willow that over him weep,
His Arm is unnerved but his Deeds remain bright
As the Stars in the dark vaulted Heaven at Night.
Oh! wake not the Hero, his Battles are o'er,
Let him rest undisturbed on Potomac's fair Shore,
On the Rivers green Border so flowery drest,
With the hearts he loved fondly, let Washington rest.

E   W

J.H. POWERS & CO. FRATERNITY PUBLISHERS, CIN⁰   ENTERED ACCORDING TO ACT OF CONGRESS BY STROBRIDGE & CO. IN THE YEAR 1873, IN THE CLERKS OFFICE OF THE U.S. DISTRICT COURT OF THE SOUTHERN DISTRICT OF OHIO.   STROBRIDGE & CO. LITH. CINCINNATI, O.

Masonic Hall, Where Washington Was Made a Mason. Fredericksburg, Va.

The Father of Our Country (his head copied from a Gilbert Stuart portrait) is depicted as a Worshipful Master of an allegorical lodge on the checkered ground floor of King Solomon's Temple. A winding stairway of three, five, and seven steps leads to the "Middle Chamber" of the temple behind him, with the five orders of architecture, Tuscan, Doric, Ionic, Corinthian, and Composite, on either side.

Wisdom, Strength, and Beauty on the column at right are the three symbolic supports of a lodge: wisdom conceives, strength supports, and beauty adorns the Mason's work. There is no evidence that Washington ever presided as Master of his lodge.

George Washington's Masonic gavel, used to lay the cornerstone of the United States Capitol, September 18, 1793.

Initiated as an Entered Apprentice Mason here in Fredericksburg Lodge in Virginia on November 6, 1752, George Washington passed to the degree of Fellowcraft the following March 3 and was raised to the Sublime Degree of Master Mason on August 4, 1753.

41

Grand Master of the Ancient Grand Lodge of Massachusetts from 1759 to 1775, Boston physician Joseph Warren spent the final weeks of his life in the eye of the revolutionary storm. It was Warren who sent William Dawes and Paul Revere to warn John Hancock and John Adams of their probable peril on April 18, 1775; in the following few weeks he was elected president pro tem of the provincial Congress, became major general in the fledgling Continental Army, and on June 17, 1775, died in the Battle of Bunker Hill, romanticized here (several years later) by painter John Trumbull. After Warren was killed, the British threw his body into an unmarked grave. Another Masonic brother, General Israel Putnam, fought alongside Warren in his shirtsleeves and survived Bunker Hill to become the most colorful figure of the Revolution.

John Jeffries was an American Freemason who supported the British cause. But he was also a member of Warren's Grand Lodge, and before fleeing Boston with the British Army he told his Masonic brothers the location of the general's grave. In this funeral procession by Boston's "Antient" Masons, Warren's exhumed body is carried to King's Chapel for reinterment.

The procession in this lithograph conforms closely to the funeral practices described in William Preston's *Illustrations of Masonry,* a ceremonial guide to English Masonry published in London in 1772. Read throughout the colonies, the book became an artist's guide to numerous similar American works. Here, the tyler with a drawn sword is followed by two deacons with rods, musicians with muffled drums and covered trumpets, and lodge members carrying flowers, herbs, and a placard with symbols. They are followed by a member carrying the Bible and Book of Constitutions on a cushion covered with a black cloth, the Worshipful Master, and, finally, pallbearers carrying the casket—just as the book prescribed, and just as it most likely happened.

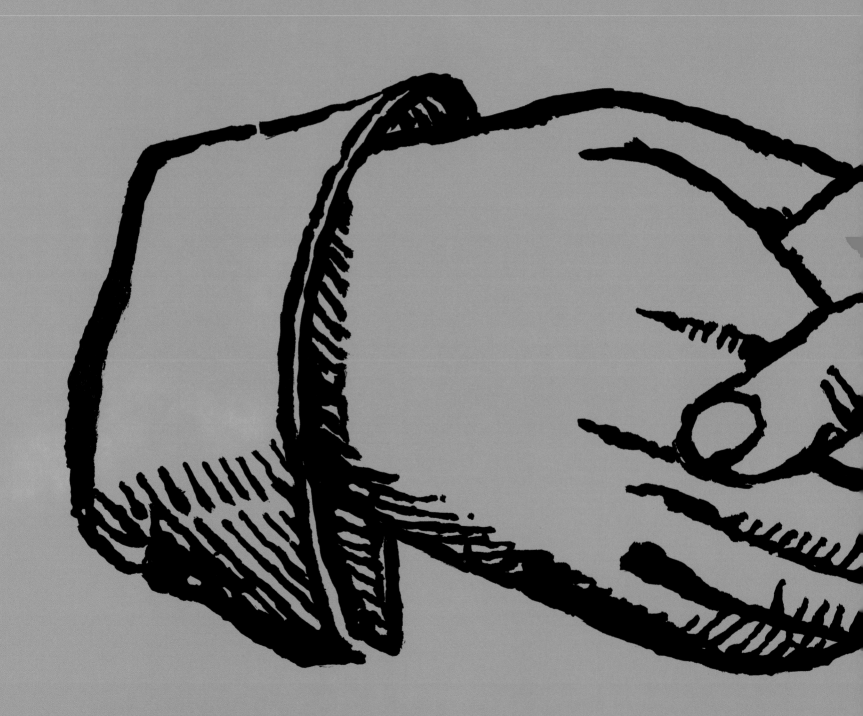

LESSONS IN STONE

From Lafayette to Pike

IN THE BEGINNING, the Scottish Rite of Freemasonry knew neither north nor south. Begun in Charleston, South Carolina, it was as indifferent to geography as to religious preference, its small founding cadre consisting almost equally of Protestants, Jews, and Catholics. During these early years, taverns were popular community social centers. Shepheard's Tavern, which also served as the local post office, already had a long history as a Masonic meeting place.

The founding father of the newly constituted Masonic Rite and Grand Commander for its first fifteen years was sixty-year-old John Mitchell, an Irish-born former deputy quartermaster general of the Continental Army with a long Masonic tradition of his own. His first Inspector General and Lieutenant Grand Commander was a young army physician, Frederick Dalcho, the son of a Prussian Freemason who served under Frederick the Great. Dalcho later gave up his medical practice to enter the ministry of the Episcopal Church. The first symbolic hand-shake, between the Marquis de Lafayette and Albert Pike in 1824, linked the prehistory of the Scottish Rite with the Masonic giant who redefined the beleaguered movement and launched it into greatness. Almost from its inception, the new fraternity faced obstacles and challenges. The anti-Masonic movement, at its most virulent in New England, turned out the lights in lodges along the whole Atlantic seaboard. Another threat was the rise of Cerneauism, a schismatic, unsanctioned degree mill which took its power—and its income—from a mimicry of the Scottish Rite. A third great challenge to the fraternity, setting brother against brother, was the American Civil War.

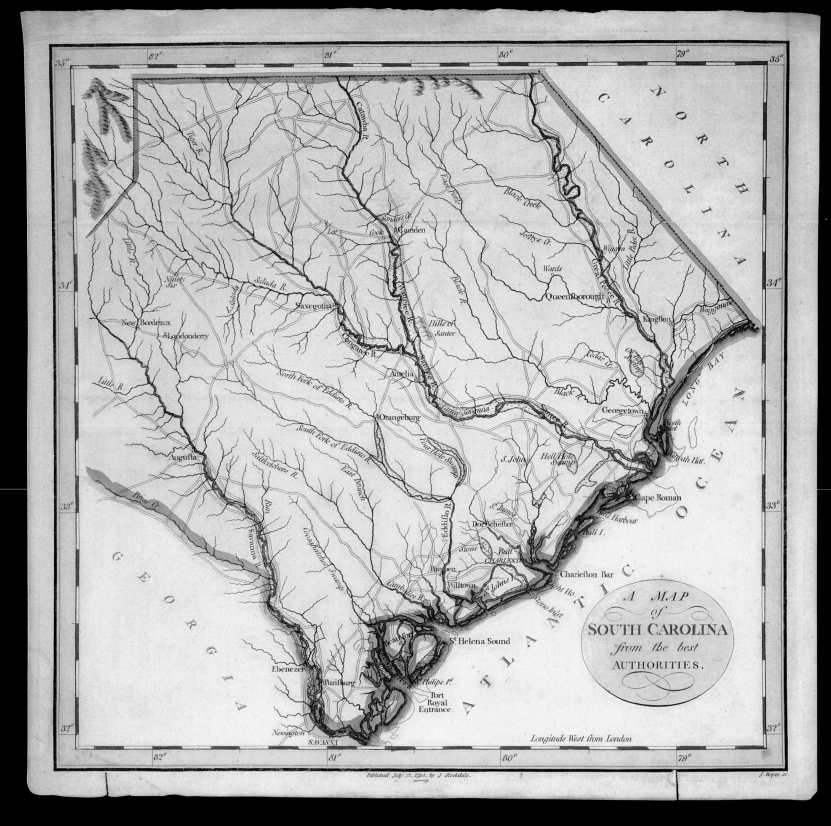

A MAP
of
SOUTH CAROLINA
from the best
AUTHORITIES.

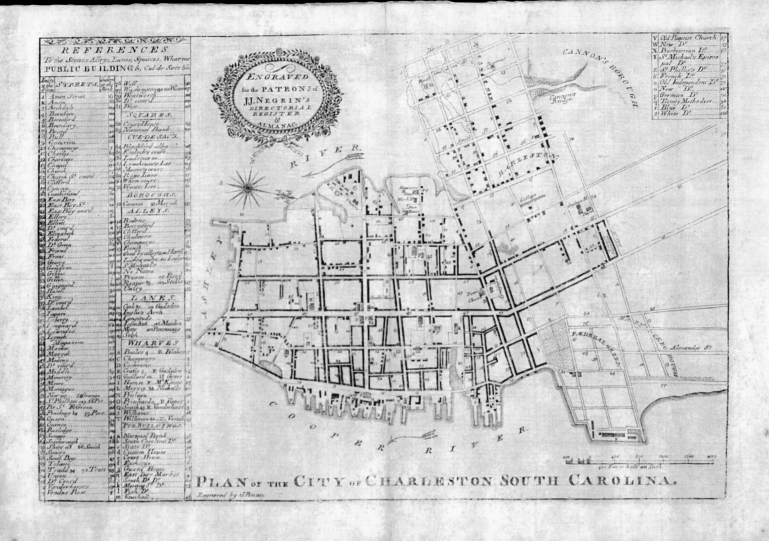

PLAN OF THE CITY OF CHARLESTON SOUTH CAROLINA.

South Carolina, birth-
place of the Scottish
Rite in America. Map
dates from the 1790s.

A plan of the city of
Charleston, South
Carolina, circa 1802.

At the corner of Church and Broad Streets in Charleston, South Carolina, stood the building originally occupied by "Mr. Shepheard's Tavern," the birthplace of the Scottish Rite; it was here that the Supreme Council, the governing body, met for the first time on May 31, 1801. The building's Masonic history began much earlier. South Carolina's first symbolic lodge met and organized at Shepheard's Tavern in 1736, and in 1783 this same building was the site of the first meeting of the Sublime Grand Lodge of Perfection, the direct antecedent of the Scottish Rite. At the time of this 1877 photo, the site's connection with Masonry in North America was already 141 years old.

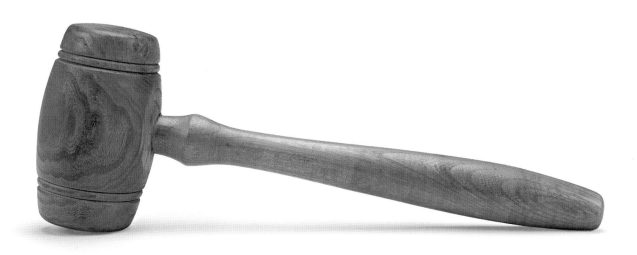

Shepheard's Tavern
interior; the Lodge of
the Temple.

Gavel made of wooden
beams from Shepheard's
Tavern.

Allyn Cox

54

Colonel John Mitchell was the first Grand Commander of the Supreme Council, presiding from 1801 to 1816. Probably initiated in Ulster, Ireland, he served as Worshipful Master of Lodge No. 8 in Charleston, as Deputy Grand Master of the Grand Lodge of South Carolina (Antients), and Inspector General for South Carolina.

Dr. Frederick Dalcho, an army physician and surgeon in Charleston, was the first recipient of the 33rd Degree of the Scottish Rite, conferred by John Mitchell (left), on May 25, 1801. Born in London of Prussian parents, Dalcho came to America after the death of his father, a Freemason who once served under Frederick the Great. The first Grand Secretary, and after Mitchell's death the second Grand Commander, he was responsible in 1817 for bringing about the union of two rival South Carolina Grand Lodges, Antients and Moderns. He later became an Episcopal priest.

The December 4, 1802, *Circular throughout the two Hemispheres* is the first printed document issued by the Supreme Council at Charleston. It traces the authority and provides an outline of the history and degrees of this new Masonic order.

Circular throughout the two Hemispheres.

---◆◆◆◆◆◆---

UNIVERSI TERRARUM ORBIS ARCHITECTONIS GLORIA AB INGENTIS.

Deus Meumque Jus.

ORDO AB CHAO.

---⌇⌇⌇⌇⌇⌇⌇---

FROM the East of the Grand and Supreme Council of the most Puissant Sovereigns, Grand Inspectors General, under the Celestial Canopy of the Zenith, which answers to the 32 deg. 45. Min. N. L.

To our Illustrious, most Valiant and Sublime Princes of the Royal Secret, Knights of K. H. Illustrious Princes and Knights, Grand Ineffable and Sublime, Free and Accepted Masons of all degrees, Ancient and Modern, over the surface of the two Hemispheres.

To all those to whom these Letters shall come :

Health, Stability and Power.

At a meeting of Sovereign Grand Inspectors General in Supreme Council, of the 33d. degree, duly and lawfully established and congregated, held at the Grand Council Chamber, on the 14th day of the 7th Month, called תשרי 5563, Anno. Lucis. 5802, and of the Christian Æra, the 10th day of October, 1802.

Union, Contentment and Wisdom.

The Grand Commander informed the Inspectors, that they were convened for the purpose of taking into consideration, the propriety of addressing circular Letters to the different Symbolic Grand Lodges, and Sublime Grand Lodges and Councils throughout the two Hemispheres, explanatory of the origin and nature of the Sublime Degrees of Masonry, and their establishment in South-Carolina.

When a resolution to that effect was immediately adopted, and a committee, consisting of the Illustrious Brethren, Doct. Frederick Dalcho, Doctor Isaac Auld and Emanuel De La Motta, Esqr. Grand Inspectors General, was appointed to draft and submit such letter to the Council at their next meeting.

At a meeting of the Sovereign Grand Inspectors General, in Supreme Council of the 33d. &c. &c. &c. on the 10th day of the 8th Month called Chisleu, 5563. A. L. 5802, and of the Christian Æra, this 4th day of December, 1802.

The

4th Degree:
Secret Master

14th Degree:
Perfection

18th Degree:
Rose Croix

Scottish Rite Masons, around the time of Napoleon's final defeat at Waterloo in 1815, are represented in watercolor drawings wearing the traditional regalia, adopting the symbolic postures, and making the signs of their respective degrees. This rare set of illustrations was sent as a gift from Brussels to the Dutch royal city of The Hague in 1817.

30th Degree:
Knight Kadosh

32nd Degree:
Prince of the Royal Secret

33rd Degree:
Grand Inspector General

Two patents issued to Dalcho by John Mitchell. (Left) Dated May 24, 1801, this patent includes English and French text, in traditional European form. (Right) The features of this patent, dated May 25, 1801, are decidedly American, its text English.

After a conflict with associates in 1823, Grand Commander Dalcho resigned his fraternal posts and gave up active leadership in Freemasonry for the remaining thirteen years of his life. But his pivotal role in the fraternity followed him to the grave.

The Dalcho Register records the earliest actions by the Supreme Council.

By the Glory of the Grand Architect of the Universe

Health Stability and Power

Lux ex Tenebris

From the East of the Grand and the most puissant Council of the Valiant Princes and Sublime Masons of the Royal Secret &c &c &c under the Celestial Canopy of the Zenith which answers to 32 degrees 47 minutes N.

To our Illustrious and most valiant Knights and princes of Free Accepted and perfect Masons of all degrees over the surface of the two Hemispheres

We Hyman Isaac Long, Grand Elect perfect and sublime Mason, Knight of the East, Prince of Jerusalem &c &c &c Patriarch Noachite, Sovereign Knight of the Sun and K. H and Deputy Inspector General over all Lodges, Chapters councils and grand Councils of the Superior degrees of Ancient and Modern Free Masonry over the surface of the two Hemispheres By Patent from B. M. Moses Cohen Deputy Grand Inspector & Prince of &c in Jamaica &c &c &c under the Special protection of the most puissant princes and in their place and stead

Do Certify and attest to all free and Valiant

The handwritten birth certificate of the Northern Jurisdiction was issued by Emmanuel de la Motta, an officer of the Supreme Council in Charleston.

This 1827 territorial agreement between the two Supreme Councils divides the jurisdictions along the Mason-Dixon Line.

HEALTH   STABILITY AND   POWER

Universi Terrarum Orbis Architectonis, per Gloriam Ingentis
Deus Meumque Jus.
Ordo ab Chao.

The Grand & Supreme Council, of the Most Puissant
Sovereigns, Grand Inspectors General of the 33°. degree,
under the C∴ C∴ of the Zenith, answering to 40°, 42′, 40″,
North Latitude, for the Northern District & Jurisdiction
of the United States of North America.
A Grand Orient well Lighted and Strong, where
reigns: Silence! Profound Peace! & Charity!

To the Grand & Supreme Council, of the Most Puissant
Sovereigns, Grand Inspectors General of the 33°. degree,
under the C∴ C∴ of the Zenith, answering to 32°, 47′, 0″,
North Latitude, for the Southern District and
Jurisdiction, of the United States of North America.
Union! Contentment! Wisdom!

Most Illustrious! Puissant! and Enlightened Brethren
At our Stated quarterly meeting on the 27th of
last June, your two Orders of the 17th May & Official
Balustrade dated 6th June with its several enclosures
were regularly laid before this Supreme Council
in reply to which, we beg leave to observe, that
it would have been answered much Sooner, had
not the necessity thereof been in a great measure precluded by the authorized private & active
correspondence of our M∴ Ill∴ Bo. Grand Secretary
Gl∴ of the H∴ E∴ with your M∴ Puis∴ Sov∴
Gd Gmmr

62

Cerneauism began earlier, and as increasingly severe anti-Masonic pressure limited fraternal activity, it filled an unmet need for Masonic ritual. When Lafayette made his farewell tour in 1824, the Cerneau organization honored him with the 33rd Degree in New York. When Lafayette arrived in Charleston, South Carolina, the Mother Council of the Scottish Rite could not honor him the way the Cerneauists had, in part because it could not recognize the degree from a rival, and in its collective mind fraudulent, Scottish Rite organization. Albert Pike finally succeeded in suppressing Cerneauism, although pockets persist to the present day.

Joseph Cerneau's 18th Degree symbol is based on earlier French designs.

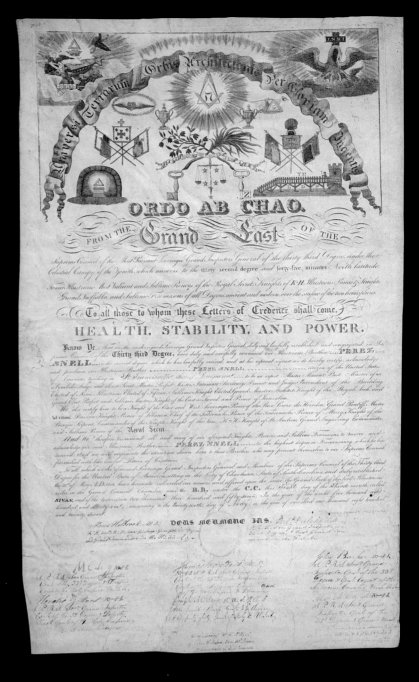

63

Cerneau's patent, issued in 1806, limited his Masonic authority to Cuba and to a non-Scottish Rite Masonic body.

Even at the height of anti-Masonic activity, the Mother Supreme Council continued to issue patents, such as this one to Perez Snell, in 1827.

William Morgan, once an apprentice stonemason, and presumably a member of the Masonic fraternity, was abducted from the jail in an upstate New York town on the night of September 12, 1826. Reportedly, Morgan was about to publish an exposé of Masonic rituals entitled *Illustrations of Masonry: By One of the Fraternity Who Has Devoted 30 Years to the Subject.*

Suffering from alcoholism and indigence, Morgan may have been motivated by revenge for professional slights and the lure of personal gain. Some sixty-nine fellow Masons were involved in his removal, but not one of them cooperated in the investigation. Although stories of his fate range from a life of secluded ease on an Ontario farm to his weighted body being thrown over Niagara Falls, he disappeared without a trace.

Andrew Jackson, a Freemason from before the start of the Supreme Council of the Scottish Rite, was elected Grand Master of the Grand Lodge of Tennessee in 1822. He became the seventh president of the United States in 1828.

With the expansion of Freemasonry came the first instances of serious anti-Masonic reaction. Starting in New England, the success of Masonry and the building of new lodges were seen as an economic and cultural threat to the declining churches. Political antagonists included a number of Federalists, and ministers preached about the problems of Masonry to increasingly receptive congregations.

By the end of Jackson's administration, charges of cronyism were rife, and he was defeated in his bid for reelection by long-time critic of Masonry, John Quincy Adams.

W. L. Stone Esqr New York

Washington 30. June 1832

Dear Sir.

I have received your kind Letter, and the elegant Volume, which you have done me the honour of addressing to me on the subject of Masonry and Anti. Masonry — Anticipating in the course of a few days a release from occupations which deprive me, at this moment of the power of perusing your work with the deep attention which the importance of the subject requires, I shall avail myself of the first hours at my disposal, to devote them to that purpose — In the mean time, I cherish the hope that the influence of this comprehensive and impartial Survey of the Masonic Institutions upon the Public mind, will contribute to induce the voluntary abandonment or renunciation of it, which I have long thought, and more firmly believe from day to day to be desirable, for the Peace and Quiet of the Community.

I am with great Respect and Esteem,

Dear Sir.

your friend and obed^t Servt

J. Q. Adams.

Adams saw Jacksonian democracy as ending a wonderful experiment in republican national life, an abandonment of the enlightened values of the American Revolution, and a dangerous turn toward the French model of mob rule. He also mistrusted Masonry as an institution, mainly for its perceived impact on American politics, where it could split votes in national elections.

Although Freemasonry had been around for generations, the Scottish Rite was still young when anti-Masonic sentiment reemerged in nineteenth-century America, sometimes in the relatively benign form of ridicule, but often as suspicion and wild rumor. In politics, the resentment became so strong it led to the creation of the Anti-Masonic Party, a short-lived but divisive force in the growing polarization of public opinion.

In the south, hostility toward Masonry became so intense that the Grand Lodge of South Carolina was unable to recruit a Protestant minister to serve as chaplain.

This 1832 letter from Adams acknowledges receipt of a book on anti-Masonry from its author, William L. Stone.

The fledgling Anti-Masonic Party receives its own share of ridicule in this cartoon commentary on the growing factionalism in American politics. Interestingly, the one issue which appears to buck the trend is abolition,

The relationship between Freemasonry and American politics was long a subject of speculation, humor, and paranoia. This Anti-Masonic political cartoon mocks the ritual with the use of arcana presumed known only to Masons. The characters on the upper right, for example, are calling out names traditionally associated in craft ritual with the assassins of Hiram Abiff, superintendent of King Solomon's Temple. This use of apparent "insider" references, some of them invented, was a common feature of such attacks.

Masonry strikes back. In this cartoon attack on the Anti-Masonic Party, the pyramid of Masonic virtues at right remains intact, rising to victory and the Perfect Light from its firm base on the Rock of Ages. The hydra of Anti-Masonry, by contrast, lies on a house in ruin, its foundation in sand, breathing a last gasp as its earlier evil aspirations twine upward toward darkness.

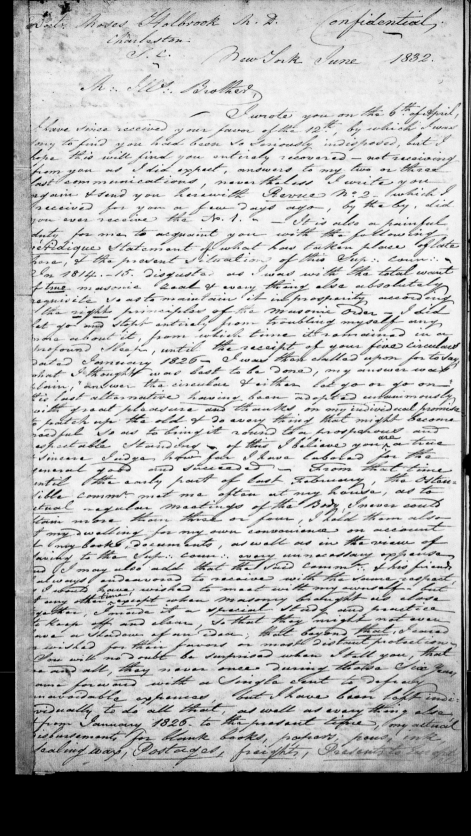

In the contest with the anti-Masonic movement for the life of the fraternity, two champions rose above the rest in their defense of the Scottish Rite. In a long correspondence, J. J. J. Gourgas, Grand Commander of the Northern Jurisdiction (above), and Moses Holbrook, his Southern counterpart, shared experiences and encouragement in the battle to preserve their common ideals.

In this "confidential" letter of June 5, 1832, Gourgas recounts the trouble, discouragement, unreimbursed expenditures, and unrewarded labors he experienced in the earliest days of his Supreme Council. Confiding that he is "disgusted…with the total want of true Masonic zeal," he puts the Northern Supreme Council into a "profound sleep" from about 1814–15 to 1826, when he will be encouraged by Holbrook to wake it up again.

DOWNFALL

OF

FREEMASONRY,

BEING

AN AUTHENTIC HISTORY OF THE RISE, PROGRESS, AND TRIUMPH

OF

ANTIMASONRY;

ALSO,

OF THE ORIGIN AND INCREASE OF

ABOLITION:

TOGETHER WITH A FAITHFUL ACCOUNT OF THE TRAVELS, DAN-
GERS, ATTACKS, DISCOVERIES, AND ESCAPES

OF THE GOVERNOR

FROM THE CUT-THROATS OF THE LODGE,

Charles R. McCrea

DURING

THE FIRST YEARS OF HIS ADMINISTRATION, IN HIS VARIOUS PE-
REGRINATIONS THROUGH THE STATE—CONTAINED IN
HIS OWN LETTERS—TO WHICH ARE PREFIXED
FAITHFUL BIOGRAPHICAL SKETCHES
OF HIS LIFE AND MY OWN,

WITH NOTES AND EXPLANATIONS,

All carefully revised by Punkin's shorthander, worked by steam from Blubberlips.

BY JONATHAN PUNKIN, ESQ.

F.P., S.P., C.C., O.A., and F. D. E. A. U. V I., &c.

PUBLISHED FOR THE EDITOR,
NEAR THE COUNCIL CHAMBERS
Unction Room,
1838.

The Governor's heroic bravery in resisting the attack of a Masonic assassin.

p 151

The Governor way-laid, and almost murdered by a royal arch-mason.

p 18

Title page and illustra-
tions from *Downfall
of Freemasonry,* one of
many anti-Masonic
tracts published during
the "Morgan Episode."

A future giant in the fraternity, Albert Pike may have found some of the initial incentive to his Masonic career when as a student of fifteen he shook hands with Lafayette during the French hero's farewell visit to America. Born and educated in the North, by the 1850s Pike was an influential lawyer and one of the richest men in Arkansas.

In March 1853, Albert Pike received the Scottish Rite degrees from General Secretary of the Supreme Council Albert Mackey. Pike is here dressed in the regalia of a Scottish Rite 32nd Degree Prince of the Royal Secret.

Brady & Co.   Washington.

Albert G. Mackey, Secretary General of the Supreme Council. A prominent Masonic historian and jurist, Mackey gave up a twenty-year career in medicine to devote his life to chronicling and leading the fraternity, serving as General Secretary of the Scottish Rite.

Of the three great challenges to the existence of the Scottish Rite in the nineteenth century—anti-Masonry, Cerneauism, and the Civil War—the last was the most threatening. Division was so deep throughout the nation that by the 1850s, national Christian denominations were split down the middle by the pressures of moral paradox and regional division.

Ironically, while South Carolina was the first state to secede and was a hotbed of anti-Union sentiment, Albert Mackey, like many in the Piedmont area, opposed secession; Albert Pike, born in the North, adopted son of the South, eventually joined the government of the Confederacy.

Rob Morris, minister-turned-businessman and co-founder of the Order of the Eastern Star, was a leading light in the "Conservator" movement to establish a uniform Grand Lodge ritual. An author and lecturer, he became known as the "poet laureate" of Freemasonry. His balanced, accessible writing in such works as *The Level, Plumb and Square,* did much to defuse the rhetoric of the anti-Masonic movement in America.

John H. Honour, an ordained minister as well as president of the Charleston Insurance and Trust Company, served as sixth Grand Commander of the Supreme Council of the Southern Jurisdiction from 1846 to 1858. He resigned his leadership (but not his membership) three years before the start of the Civil War.

73

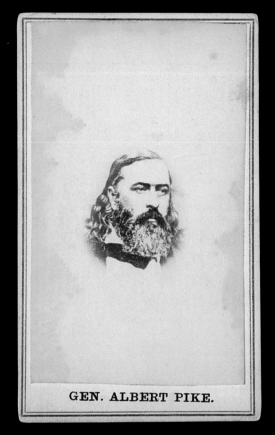

GEN. ALBERT PIKE.

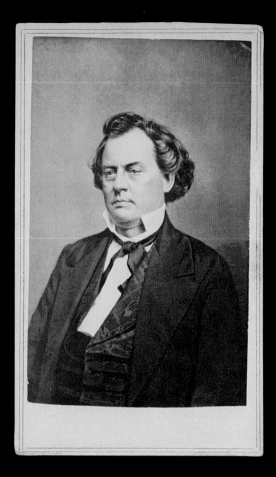

74

Albert Pike, as a general in the Army of the Confederacy. Pike's new job drew on his expertise in Indian affairs, involving him in an effort to co-opt Indian tribes to help control the lower Mississippi Valley and gain a strategic Confederate Western foothold. If this attempt had succeeded, instead of resulting in such tragedies as the Battle of Pea Ridge, the Civil War might have gone on much longer.

The war was filled with stories and images of men from the same fraternities—sometimes even the same families—belonging to opposing armies. Under the pressures of anti-Masonry and the Civil War, the Scottish Rite was driven into a more internalized reality.

Variously secretary of the treasury of the United States, a Confederate general, and governor of Georgia, secessionist Howell Cobb became an active member of the Southern Supreme Council in early 1860.

A United States congressman and then senator from Georgia, Robert Toombs became the Confederacy's first secretary of state as well as a general in Lee's army, noted for his defense of Burnside's Bridge at the Battle of Antietam in 1862. Toombs was elected to the Supreme

Council in 1872. Like Pike, he began his career as a lawyer and member of the Whig party. Years later, he recalled Pike's observation in 1856 that "the Masons are trying to keep the Union from being broken up."

MASONIC WAR CERTIFICATE.

To all Free and Accepted Masons to whom this may come,

WE SEND FRATERNAL GREETING:

Know Ye, that the bearer hereof, Bro. *Fera Mihlotzky* now serving in ~~Company~~ *Lieut Colonel, Jaeger Regiment Illinois Volunteers,* under the command of Colonel _____ is a Master Mason in good standing and a member of *Lafayette* Lodge No. *18,* at *Chicago* County of *Cook* Illinois, and is fraternally commended to the care, sympathy and good fellowship of all good Master Masons and Master's Lodges, in whatever situation, condition or place the fortune or casualties of war or military service may find him.

Let all concerned take due notice hereof and govern themselves accordingly.

Given under my hand and the seal of the Grand Lodge, Ancient, Free and Accepted Masons, at the city of Springfield, State of Illinois, this, the *26th* day of *July* A. D. *1861,* A. L. *5861,* and of the Independence of the United States the eighty-*fifth*

HARMAN G. REYNOLDS,
Grand Secretary.

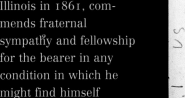

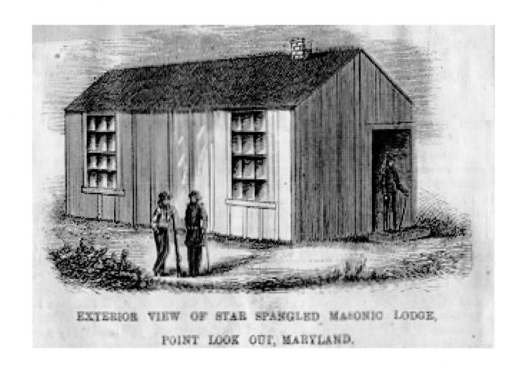

EXTERIOR VIEW OF STAR SPANGLED MASONIC LODGE,
POINT LOOK OUT, MARYLAND.

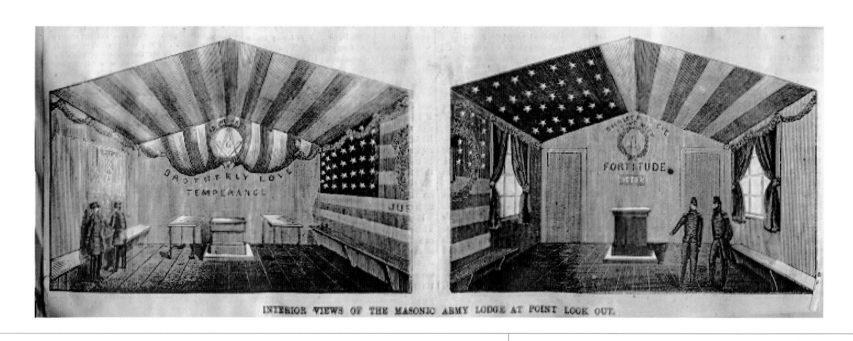

INTERIOR VIEWS OF THE MASONIC ARMY LODGE AT POINT LOOK OUT.

A Northern presence in the Southern Jurisdiction, this Masonic army lodge at Point Lookout, Maryland, was erected and decorated by Masons with the 2nd Regiment of New Hampshire Volunteers. The local newspaper observed, "Only men of the highest character are admitted as members of the Lodge, which exerts a very salutary influence."

Old Home of Albert Pike Little Rock ark

At a time when the country's values were changing with regional conflict and rapid urbanization, the log cabin—whether Pike's or Abraham Lincoln's—became an icon of America's vanishing simplicity. Toward the end of the Civil War, Pike retired to this rustic home in the Arkansas wilderness where he continued his revision of the ritual of the Scottish Rite degrees. He set the terms and conditions of this branch of the Masonic fraternity for the next 150 years.

The home Pike left behind. This plantation mansion house in Little Rock symbolizes a vanished era.

OVERLEAF
Charleston, South Carolina, 1865: An ending, and a new beginning.

1860–1921

A NEW FOUNDATION

From Pike to Cowles

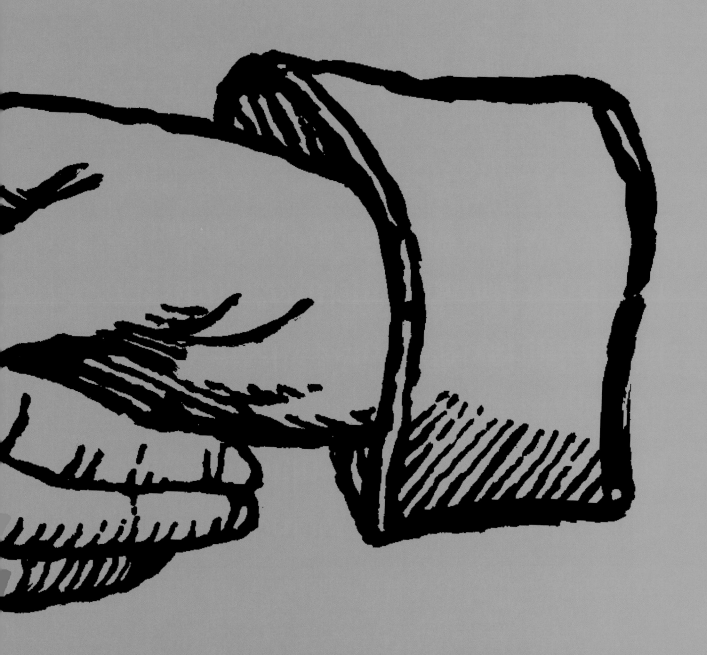

THE LEADERSHIP of three powerful but different personalities—Albert Pike, James D. Richardson, and John H. Cowles—defined and dominated the center years of the Scottish Rite's first two centuries in America. Pike was a philosopher whose mystic vision revitalized and refocused the values, the symbols, the legends, and the interpretation of the Scottish Rite. Through great intellect and heroic force of character, he turned his beloved institution away from the loss and sorrow of the past and once more claimed a bright and self-renewing future. 🤝 Richardson was a visionary as well, but his special gift was organization. A scholar and preservationist, he was also a politician skilled in working with constituents and running campaigns. His role was to make tangible Pike's vision and translate those values into action. 🤝 Cowles was the quintessential manager, a businessman in the era of big business, who succeeded Richardson at the start of the Roaring Twenties. 🤝 The beginning of the

Pike incumbency is separated by sixty years and a world of change from the installation of John Cowles. But like all the other links in this chain, they are connected by a handshake. This one took place in the library of Pike's home in the original House of the Temple in Washington, D.C. near the end of Pike's long tenure as Grand Commander and over three decades before Cowles himself assumed that same high office.

The visionary who redefined the Scottish Rite, Albert Pike poses in full Masonic regalia near the start of his long tenure as Grand Commander, which stretched from shortly after the Civil War to the threshold of the twentieth century. Note the Grand Commander's jewel of the double-headed eagle suspended beneath the number 33 framed by an equilateral triangle.

Pike's ceremonial sword and scabbard and his 33rd Degree collar.

In 1849, transplanted
Northerner Albert Pike
appeared totally at home
among the antebellum
Southern aristocracy.
Handsome, tall, exuding
an assured, rawboned
confidence, he appears
with fellow Masons
(from left) Charles L.
Elliot, John A. Haggerty,
William T. Porter, and
J. R. Clark. Pike is on
the far right.

Daniel in the lion's den.
Pike arrived in the
capital of the recently
reunited nation in the
hope of continuing a
distinguished career in
the practice of law. But

The credentials on Pike's
first postwar business
card in Washington are
a hopeful résumé of his
earlier life.

Pike, like the country, was determined to rebuild his life.

A Pike jewel and double-headed eagle jewel.

Once one of the wealthiest men in Little Rock, with the largest private library in the South, Pike had lost everything, including the plantation house.

91

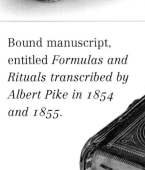

Bound manuscript, entitled *Formulas and Rituals transcribed by Albert Pike in 1854 and 1855*.

Pike's *Morals and Dogma* (far left) was begun in New Orleans, Louisiana, as "Lectures of All the Degrees" and completed during his self-imposed exile in rural Arkansas at Greasy Cove, on the Little Missouri River, during the last year of the Civil War. The lectures, once part of the ritual, were omitted in subsequent revisions and printed separately. The resulting volume revitalized the Scottish Rite by codifying and expounding its philosophy.

Grand Commander Albert Pike near the end of the century. Pike's work was based on a broad knowledge of ancient religions and mythologies and his wide reading of earlier Masonic writings, especially the older rituals, which he collected in the volume at left. Through the combination of his formidable literary gifts and a finely honed sense of the dramatic, he emerged as the premier authority on the Scottish Rite ritual.

King David Kalakaua of Hawaii stands for a formal portrait in his Masonic sash, jewel, and apron. Following his 1874 election to the throne, the king visited lodges in Washington, Boston, New York, and Chicago, as well as in Europe, remaining active in the brotherhood for the rest of his life. He died in San Francisco in 1891 after a Shrine reception in his honor, which he attended against doctor's orders.

Although disciplined by Pike for a breach of Scottish Rite protocol in 1881, the king honored the Grand Commander in this lavish, courtly letter three years later.

Iolani Palace. Honolulu
March 26. 1884.

Very Ill∴ Bro∴
Albert Pike 33°
Grand Com∴ of Sup∴ Council
33° A∴ & A∴ S∴ R∴ S∴ Jur∴ of U.S.A.

Dear Sir and Brother

Being deeply moved by various considerations, prominent among which is the World-wide fame of your virtues and services to our beloved Order, as well as the acknowledgement due to you from me, and the Masonic brethern of these Islands of the mid-ocean, for establishing here the Scottish Rite, with all its accessories and gradations of Masonic excellence and beauty; it affords me much pleasure to offer you, for your acceptance, the Diploma and Insignia of the Grand Officer of Our Royal Order of the "Crown of Hawaii"

Praying the Grand Architect of the Universe to have you ever in His Holy Keeping, I am

Illustrious Sir and Brother
Fraternally and truly yours

Kalakaua 33°

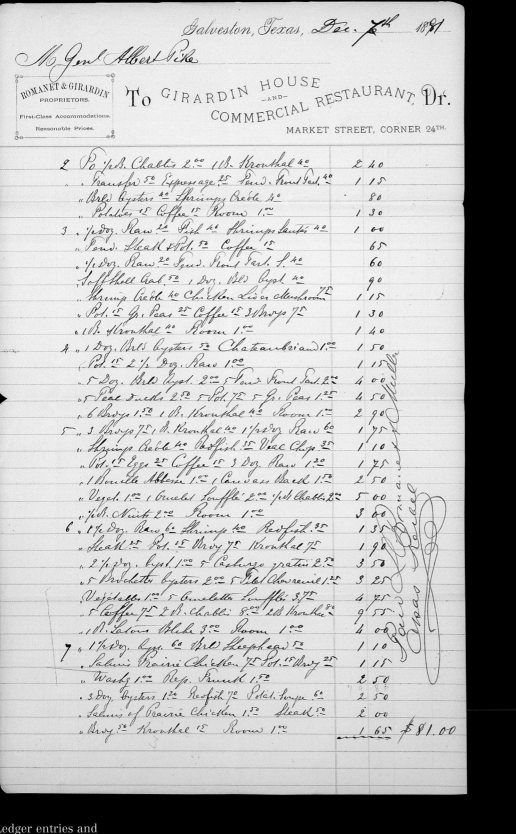

Galveston, Texas, Dec. 7th 1891

M. Genl Albert Pike

ROMANET & GIRARDIN
PROPRIETORS.
First-Class Accommodations.
Reasonable Prices.

To GIRARDIN HOUSE
—and—
COMMERCIAL RESTAURANT, Dr.
MARKET STREET, CORNER 24TH.

$81.00

Ledger entries and
receipts from Pike's

The faces of fellowship, from Albert Pike's personal photo album. By the 1870s, the resurgence of the Scottish Rite had to be good news for former Civil War photographer Mathew Brady, whose Washington studio on Pennsylvania Avenue

A Masonic picnic, circa 1870, is recorded by the new Stereopticon camera for three-dimensional viewing.

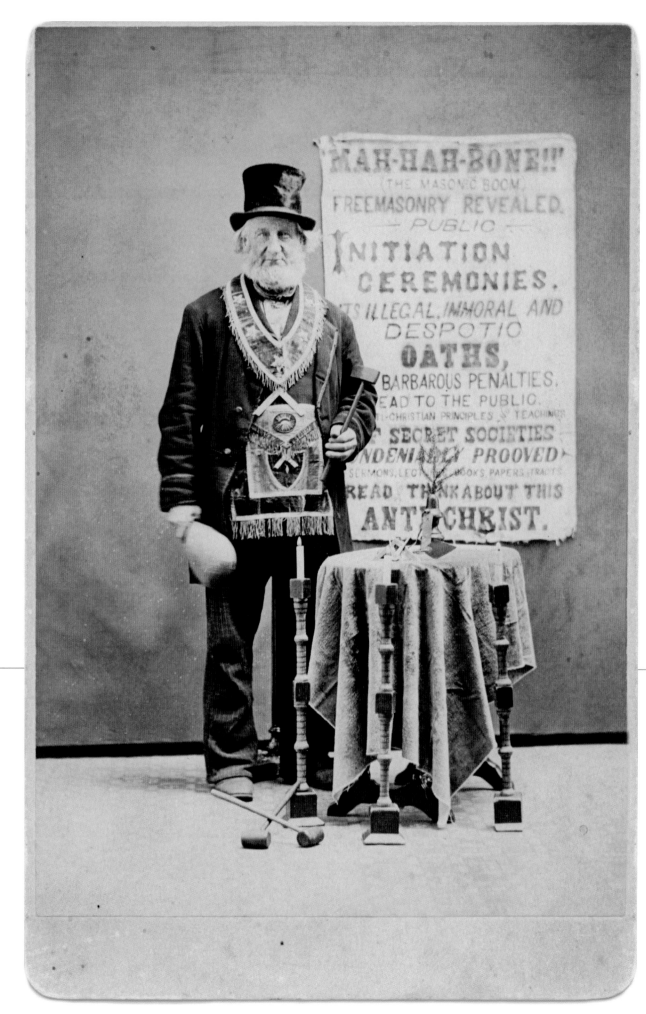

An affable, slightly sheepish-looking anti-Mason, circa 1870, dressed in apparently legitimate regalia, hoping to titillate the buying public's appetite for all things Masonic with a lurid menu of manufactured evidence against the "anti-Christ."

VOL. XI.-No. 275

JUNE 14, 1882

Price, 10 Cents.

"What fools these Mortals be!"
MIDSUMMER-NIGHTS DREAM

Puck

PUBLISHED BY
KEPPLER & SCHWARZMANN.

NEW YORK
TRADE MARK REGISTERED 1878.

OFFICE No. 21 - 23 WARREN ST.

"ENTERED AT THE POST OFFICE AT NEW YORK, AND ADMITTED FOR TRANSMISSION THROUGH THE MAILS AT SECOND CLASS RATES."

THE MIGHTY MEETING OF THE MASONS.

When one's a Mason, However snide,
He must aprons place on And collars wide.

Then he'll pass from "Labor"—Which is swopping grips,
With his "brother" neighbor, To "Refreshment"—nips.

—Conspirators' Chorus in "la Fille de Mme. Angot"—New Version

Anti-Masonic attacks, such as this cartoon from the cover of *Puck,* a leading nineteenth-century magazine of American social satire, produced a vital, if accidental, benefit for the Scottish Rite. By reducing some of the earlier perceptions of social advantage in becoming a Freemason, they forced the institution toward a greater focus on the spiritual and intrinsic qualities of fraternal life and experience.

LES MYSTÈRES DE LA **FRANC-MAÇONNERIE**

par **LÉO TAXIL**

P. Méjanel

LETOUZEY & ANÉ, Éditeurs, 17, rue du Vieux-Colombier, Paris

French hoaxer Leo Taxil's book, *Les mystères de la Franc-Maçonnerie* (The Mysteries of Free-masonry), was published in several languages.

Author Leo Taxil (pseudonym for Gabriel Antoine Jogand-Pagès) was an anti-Mason who became infamous for inventing quotations which he attributed to Albert Pike.

Simultaneously turning out anti-Catholic and anti-Masonic tracts under different aliases, he played one faction against the other for profit, with occasional detours into pornography. Eventually he confessed to his forgeries, saying he hoped revealing the elaborate hoax would shame the Vatican into disavowing its antipathy to things Masonic. He must have been disappointed. In the 1884 encyclical, *Humanum Genus,* Leo XIII continued a 150-year papal tradition, influenced by Taxil's lurid fabrications, by launching yet another jolting attack on Free-masonry. Today, more than a century after his admission, the most outrageous of Taxil's forgeries, including *"Oui, Lucifer est Dieu ..."* ("Yes, Lucifer is God ..."), remain the sine qua non of anti-Masonic litera-ture. "The truth is not hard to kill," Mark Twain later observed, "but a lie, well told, is immortal."

Bogus representations of Masonic rituals, includ-ing blood sacrifice and devil worship, as depicted in these illustrations of a Taxil text, became a common element in cari-catures and attacks on the Scottish Rite.

Two Masons as Knights
of the Council of Kadosh,
which govern the 19th
through 30th Degrees,
and a Knight Kadosh
ceremonial sword.

The dress of these Masons from a country lodge of the 1870s offers a somber contrast to the style and flourish of the Knights Kadosh of the same period.

Prince Hall Masonry began the year before the American Revolution, and twenty-six years before the Scottish Rite, when fifteen black Bostonians, including one named Prince Hall, were raised as Master Masons within the laws and customs of the Grand Lodge of England.

Pike supplied Prince Hall Freemasons with his personal copies of Scottish Rite rituals, including *Morals and Dogma*, but he opposed the absorption or recognition of Masons of color by the Southern Jurisdiction.

A white-haired, nearly spectral Albert Pike (hatless, at lower right of banner) attends a cornerstone ceremony for the Cathedral of the Scottish Rite in Washington, D.C., June 7, 1888, three years before his death.

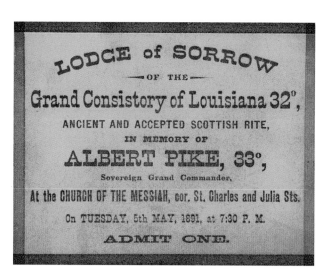

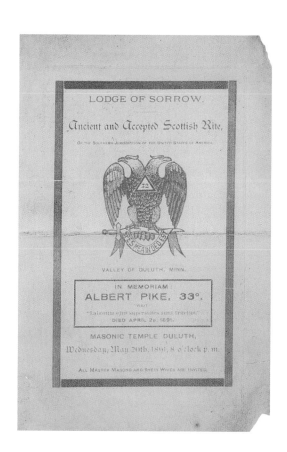

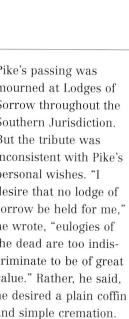

Pike's passing was mourned at Lodges of Sorrow throughout the Southern Jurisdiction. But the tribute was inconsistent with Pike's personal wishes. "I desire that no lodge of sorrow be held for me," he wrote, "eulogies of the dead are too indiscriminate to be of great value." Rather, he said, he desired a plain coffin and simple cremation.

Pike's body lay in state for five days in the House of the Temple, then for another two days at the Scottish Rite Cathedral (shown here) on G Street NW. At midnight on April 9, 1891, the Kadosh funeral service was said at Washington's historic First Congregational Church, an early Abolitionist stronghold where Howard University had been founded just a generation before. This venue lent fitting symmetry—and perhaps some spiritual clemency —to the career of the former Confederate general who helped restore Freemasonry as one of the great institutions of a wounded nation. Another service was held for his children the following day at the Episcopal Church of the Ascension, again in the presence of an enormous crowd. His remains were interred at Oak Hill Cemetery in Washington, D.C., for the next three decades.

City of Washington, D. C.
February 11th 1891

Know all men by these Presents that I, Albert Pike, have this day given and do hereby give grant and convey unto Frederick Webber, as Secretary General of the Supreme Council of the 33:. of the Ancient and Accepted Scottish Rite of Free Masonry of the Southern Jurisdiction of the United States, in trust for the said Supreme Council, the following articles of personal property, that is to say:

The colossal meerschaum pipe, presented to me by Bro:. William S. Roose;

The large, finely-carved meerschaum pipe, ornamented with gold by Bro:. Edward Williams, bought by me at Memphis and now in the glass case in the museum;

The finely-carved pipe of Maltese meerschaum, representing a Chamois-hunt, which took the gold medal at the Paris Exposition and was given to me by Bro:. Dorn;

The large meerschaum pipe surmounted by a silver statuette of Germania; the plain bowl of which was purchased, for $180.00, by brethren in Baltimore, and mounted by them and presented to me some twenty years ago;

The two red-stone, Indian-pipes, one of which I have had since 1861; the other was given to me by Bro:. Henry Lippincott, U. S. Army;

The bamboo tobacco-box given me by Bro:.

Robin McDaniel;

The silver mouth-piece of a Narghile, now in the glass case of the museum; the silver bowl of the same for a Censer; the Japanese cane given me by Bro:. McRitchie; the diamond-willow cane, given me by Bro:. Freeman of Elk Point in Dakota; the cane of many pieces of wood, given me by Bro:. Eugene Grissom; the cane covered with split reed, sent me by Bro:. James R. Hayden; the silver ink-stand given me by Bro:. Frederick Webber; the little Japanese pipe, sheath and pouch given me forty years ago by William T. Porter; the bust of myself made by Vinnie Ream; the crayon-portrait of John R. McDaniel; and that of myself, now in the Library; and my portrait painted by Charles Elliott;

And I have, to-day, made actual delivery of all the same, unto Bro:. Frederick Webber to make this conveyance absolute, for sufficient consideration by me received from the Supreme Council.

Given under my hand the day and date aforesaid.

Albert Pike

Witness:
Ashton f. A. White.

Albert Pike's will.

The Scottish Rite Temple
in Charleston, South
Carolina, reflects the
move toward grander
lodgings. Like its counterpart in Washington, D.C.,
this elegant edifice was
an existing structure
acquired, not built, to
house the brotherhood
and its expanding
aspirations.

Rapid succession. The first House of the Temple in Washington, D.C., from 1870 to 1900, was in a row of connected brownstones at Third and E Streets, NW. Between April 1891 and July 1894, a period of just thirty-nine months, three Grand Commanders —Pike, Batchelor, and Tucker—all died in this building.

Albert Pike's immediate successor, James C. Batchelor, a Canadian-born Alabaman, had been Lieutenant Grand Commander of the Supreme Council since 1878. Batchelor's Masonic career parallels Pike's; once a Confederate Army captain and prisoner of war, he outlived his mentor long enough to preside at only one council session, in October of 1892, dying just nine months later.

Phillip C. Tucker followed Batchelor as Grand Commander in 1893, then died in July of the following year.

Despite the forbidding iron fence, the library in the old House of the Temple accumulated Masonic titles so fast they could not all be properly cataloged. By 1894 this room was full, and some 5,000 additional volumes were shelved elsewhere in the building. The Supreme Council Library, antici-

pating Andrew Carnegie's benevolence, was the first library, free and open to the public, in Washington, D.C. To complete the chaos of this transitional era, on the day after the death of Grand Commander Tucker, his old friend Dr. Thomas Hatch, the librarian, died as well.

Inner room, outer world. Following the death of Albert Pike, the Scottish Rite underwent a dramatic transition that paralleled changes in the country's relationship to the outside world at the century's end. Even as America expanded to continental borders, the country's focus was still inward, healing in the aftermath of the Civil War and relatively untested in the new poli-

tics of internationalism. The colonial empires of Europe continued to expand, with Britain nearing the height of its power and Germany trying to enlarge its holdings in Africa and exerting new influence in South America. Despite itself, the United States was to be tested in this great contest.

A metaphor for the transition is in these two views of the Supreme Council lodge room in the old Washington House of the Temple. In the first, taken about 1895, the room is dominated by a massive, fabric-wrapped proscenium dividing it at the center. Dark and heavy curtains frame the stage, a protective shroud that at once enhances and obscures the symbols of great Masonic mysteries

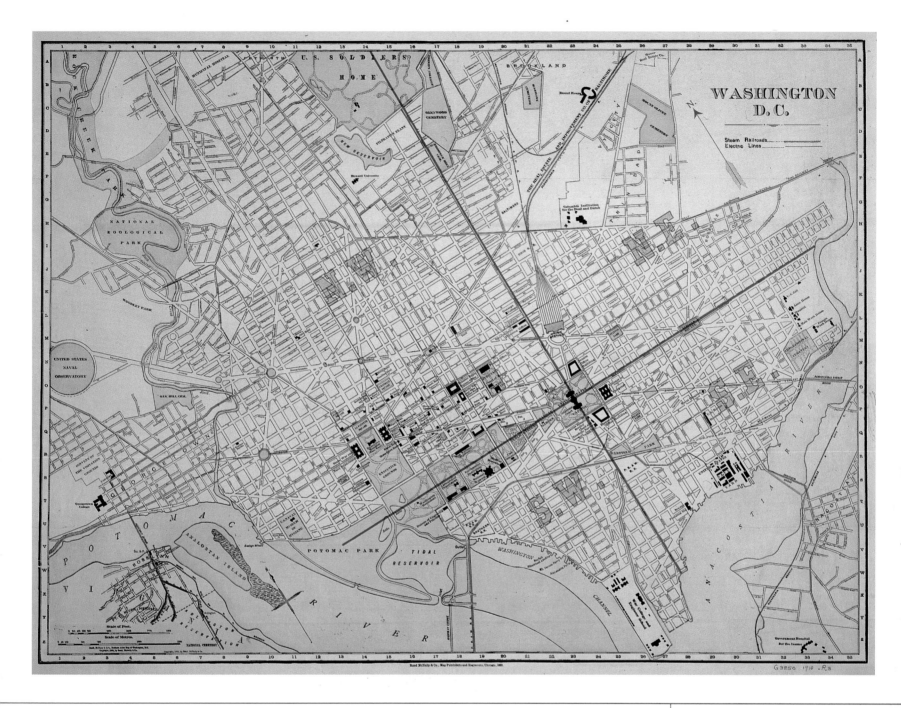

contained within. The country's flag and the Masonic banner are relegated to positions on opposite sides of the room from each other and well beyond the focal center of the tableau.

The second photograph shows the same room just ten years later. Although the architecture is unchanged, the symbolic use of this ritual space now serves a far

different vision. The massive fabric room divider is gone, and with it the heavy drapery above and beside the stage. The new boundaries to the stage are now the prominently displayed American flag and the Supreme Council banner. With America's newly found confidence and patriotism, the country's flag has become a valued symbol of the Scottish Rite for the dawning twentieth century.

The defining event of that ten-year spread was the Spanish-American War. When it was over, the young country's horizons had expanded to embrace the globe.

Like the Scottish Rite and like the United States, the Nation's Capital in 1900 was a work in progress.

A California judge, Thomas Caswell was seventy at the time of his investiture as head of the Supreme Council in October 1895. He brought a breadth and variety of experience to his role as Grand Commander, having worked as a reporter in Cooperstown, New York, studied law in Arkansas, prospected for gold in the rush of '49, and practiced as an attorney in frontier Nevada. He appears here in the regalia of a Grand High Priest (York Rite) of Royal Arch Masons for the state of Nevada.

Caswell is front and center in this 1895 photo of Scottish Rite leaders. In the back row, directly behind him, is future Grand Commander Richardson. The last person on the right in the back row is George F. Moore, who will directly succeed Richardson.

Members of the Supreme Council. Grand Commander Caswell, wearing the jewel of his office, is in the center of the front row.

The six years of Caswell's incumbency included a severe economic depression and the Spanish-American War. But for the Scottish Rite it was a time of growing membership and new prosperity.

119

Two years after leading these Rough Riders to a decisive victory at the top of Cuba's San Juan Hill in 1898, Colonel Theodore Roosevelt of New York (at center, below flag, with thumbs hooked in his garrison belt), a long-time Mason, will be nominated to the vice presidency of the United States. His party will lose the election, but TR's time will come.

William McKinley, president of the United States during the Spanish-American War, and a member of Eagle Lodge, No. 431, Canton, Ohio, poses proudly in his Masonic apron beside the symbolic square, compasses, and Bible.

Lt. General Nelson A. Miles won the Congressional Medal of Honor in the Civil War battle of Chancellorsville and commanded an army corps of 26,000 men at the age of twenty-five. On the Western frontier he led campaigns against Sitting Bull, Crazy Horse, Chief Joseph, Geronimo, and Natchez. At the time of the Spanish-American War, he was Senior Commanding Officer of the United States Army; raised in 1888, he received the Scottish Rite degrees in Albert Pike Consistory in Washington, D.C.

Lt. General Arthur MacArthur, Jr., another Civil War Congressional Medalist (for heroism at Missionary Ridge), entered Magnolia Lodge No. 60, Little Rock, Arkansas, while a captain, in 1879. The father of General Douglas A. MacArthur, he served as military governor of the Philippines at the end of the Spanish-American War, where he was an antagonist of fellow Mason William Howard Taft, future president and later chief justice of the United States.

At Destiny's Gate. The Spanish-American War launched the United States into the twentieth century with a new optimism and suddenly expanded horizons, reflected here in the tangible pride and determination of future Grand Commander, Captain John Cowles (seated on right), Company H, 1st Kentucky Volunteers.

Cowles in mufti during that same period.

Cowles in the army in Ponce, Puerto Rico, during the Spanish-American War.

Cowles's commanding officer, Colonel John B. Castleman, was also a Scottish Rite Mason.

Masons of every rite were prominent in the Spanish-American War. Masonic jewels and medallions represent the rank and other honors of their owners. These are from an outstanding collection now displayed in the John H. Cowles Room, House of the Temple, Washington, D.C. They reflect the involvement of Freemasons in this pivotal conflict.

Emilio Aguinaldo and author Charles S. Lobingier in Rose Croix attire, in the Philippines around 1925. Aguinaldo, the George Washington of his country, wore a black bow tie for almost fifty years in symbolic mourning of United States annexation.

Lobingier founded the Scottish Rite in the Philippines in 1907, becoming a Deputy of the Supreme Council there for three years and later holding a comparable position in China. The first 33rd Degree Freemason to receive the Scottish Rite's Grand Cross (1925), he became the first Intendant General for the Far East.

Cowles speaks at a lodge meeting in Puerto Rico in the 1930s. Cowles's return, thirty years after the war, was not as a conqueror but as a brother.

125

Raised again in 1900–01, Albert Pike emerged in epic scale consistent with his role in the evolution of the brotherhood. Sculpted and cast by Gaetano Trentanove of Florence, on its eighteen-foot red granite pedestal the twelve-foot statue rises as high as a three-story building. While the sculpture was being completed in the artist's Washington studio, the massive base was assembled at what today is known as Judiciary Square.

Gone but not forgotten. The Albert Pike Memorial was erected on land set aside by Congress and dedicated in 1901, ten years after his death and in the centennial year of the Scottish Rite. Although unrelated to Pike's role in the Civil War, a century later it remains the only statue of a former Confederate soldier or administrator ever permitted on public land in the Nation's Capital.

Centennial memorabilia
include this nonpostal
commemorative Pike
stamp, calendars bearing
his image, and related
artifacts attesting to
Pike's continuing ascen-
dancy in the Masonic
pantheon.

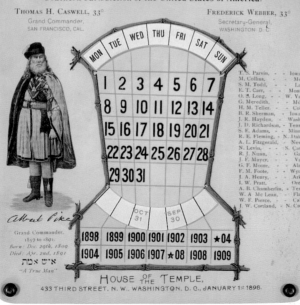

Members of the Supreme
Council and brother
Masons from all over
the United States gather
in solemn tribute at the
dedication and unveiling.

ART GALLERY

night
y Festival
ton May 23, 06

133

Masonic May festivals continued a centuries-old British tradition of holiday fairs and camp meetings. Such events offered a modern advantage in shifting the venue of the fraternity to permit the participation of women.

134

In 1874, James D. Richardson, 31, was Eminent Commander of the Knights Templar (York Rite) in Murfreesboro, Tennessee. A future congressman, he was one of Albert Pike's most influential successors.

Richardson, a Civil War veteran, was still a congressman from Tennessee in 1900 when he succeeded to Albert Pike's mantle as the next major figure to become Grand Commander of the Southern Jurisdiction. (There were three other leaders between them.)

Richardson with the Supreme Council at the start of his administration. No less a visionary than Albert Pike, who had brought him into the Supreme Council in 1885, Richardson focused his political skills on organization, membership, and the building of an institutional consensus. During his time in Congress the MacMillan Commission gave impetus to the beautification of American cities, a movement which had particular impact on Washington in the landscape architecture of Rock Creek Park and in similar innovations by Frederick Law Olmsted in Boston and New York. With the rise of great mansions and dramatic new public buildings, the growth of America's cities was driven by a fresh sense of aesthetic unity in balance with nature. As an architect in the middle of this major progressive movement, Richardson selected the design for the ambitious new House of the Temple, the most visible expression of the aspirations, philosophy, and successes of the Scottish Rite in the new century.

#19.

Richardson at Scottish
Rite headquarters in
Washington, D.C., in
1904. To his left, without
a hat, is Charles E.
Rosenbaum, who played
a key role in the building
of the future House of
the Temple.

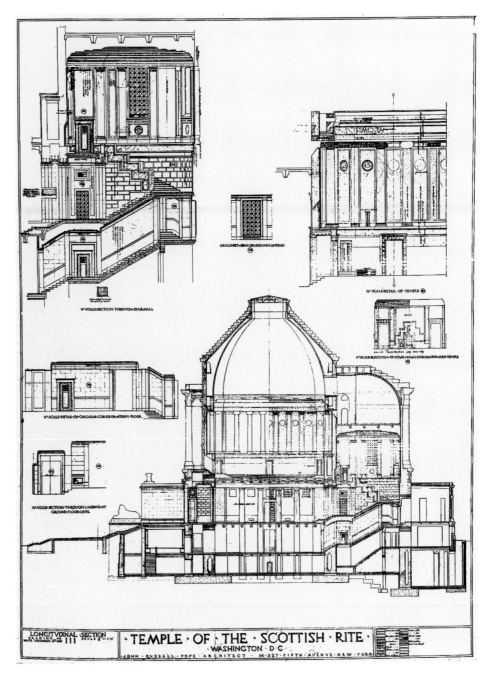

One of the Seven Wonders of the Ancient World, the mausoleum at Halikarnassos (circa 352 BC) is associated with the roots of Western architectural history. In designing the House of the Temple, architect John Russell Pope (lower left) drew on reconstructions of the classic edifice by historians and archaeologists, based on surviving contemporary descriptions of its dimensions, columns, and stepped pyramidal roof supporting a quadriga. "Roman architects of two thousand years ago would prefer [it] to any of their own work," a prominent critic said of the new structure in 1921.

Charles Edward Rosenbaum (upper left), who held a succession of key positions on the Supreme Council during the course of this construction project, initially favored an architect whose design was based on the Taj Mahal. Later, however, Rosenbaum formed a close working relationship with Pope.

Pope's early renderings of the House of the Temple. A near-perfect expression of Masonic mysticism and ideals— and of Grand Commander Richardson's unifying vision for the fraternity's future—the new building remained in harmony with its setting and with the spirit of its times through the twentieth century and into the new millennium.

Groundbreaker. At nine o'clock in the morning of May 31, 1911, the 110th anniversary of the Supreme Council, Richardson turns the first shovelful of earth at the site of Washington's monumental new House of the Temple.

INDIANA LIMESTONE COMPANY
BEDFORD, INDIANA

RAND TOWER
PLYMOUTH BUILDING
HENNEPIN AVE. AND SIXTH ST.

MINNEAPOLIS, MINNESOTA

June 14, 1930.

Dr. W. B. Roberts,
La Salle Bldg.,
Minneapolis, Minn.

Dear Doctor:

I am enclosing two photographs, which I know will be
of interest to you - one showing two mammoth blocks
from which the sphinx of Scottish Rite Cathedral,
Washington, D. C. was carved. The other photograph
shows the quarry from which these blocks came. I
happened to be at the quarry at the time they were
taken out, and also when the large columns were being
quarried and turned, and believe me, they were some
chunks.

Yours very sincerely,

Wm. V. Grubbs

2 Encls.

The NATION'S BUILDING STONE

View of the PBM Quarry, of Indiana Limestone Company, Bedford, Indiana, and the Select Buff Indiana Oolithic limestone blocks that were cut there for the sphinx statues now guarding the entrance to the House of the Temple. Described in the correspondence as "some chunks," each stone weighs approximately 215,000 pounds.

JUNE 30, 1913.

Architectural progress
photographs by Harris
and Ewing were shot
every two weeks between
the groundbreaking and
dedication of the House
of the Temple.

144

Richardson wore this jewel of a Grand Commander, Albert Pike's nine-point, gem-encrusted starburst.

When Richardson took office at the start of the century, membership in the Scottish Rite stood at 10,000 and degrees were bestowed one man at a time. Pike himself had seldom staged the degree ceremony in large rooms, preferring to confer degrees in a relaxed and private setting. Under Richardson's leadership the ritual flourished as a theatrical event for the mass induction of candidates. By using a proscenium stage instead of a lodge room, Richardson produced degree ceremonies as plays, with casts of ritualists. Candidates entered into the experience of the ritual as if they were watching *Othello* or *Henry IV,* an innovation which changed everything. Membership exploded.

By the time young Charles Lindbergh received his degrees in St. Louis, a year before his 1927 conquest of the Atlantic, the Scottish Rite, Southern Jurisdiction, had grown beyond 300,000.

Apron worn by Grand Master J. Claude Keiper of the District of Columbia at the cornerstone ceremony.

Masonic moment. The Reverend William T. Snyder offers the invocation at the cornerstone ceremony of the new House of the Temple on October 18, 1911, two days after the opening of the biennial session of the Supreme Council.

Reading room of the
new library. Throughout
the main rooms of the
structure, Pope super-
vised the custom design
of all the light fixtures,
lamps, and furniture,
down to the smallest
ornamental detail.

Offices of the Grand
Secretary General and
the office of the Grand
Commander.

ROOSEVELT THE MASTER MASON

© 1912
J.L. PHELPS
SPOKANE

Hero of San Juan Hill, Theodore Roosevelt succeeded to the presidency of the United States upon the death of fellow Mason William McKinley in 1901, then won another four years in 1904. Here he visits a lodge in Spokane, Washington, in 1912. The first president known to campaign in Masonic regalia, the former Rough Rider maintained his interests as big game hunter, historian, adventurer, writer, and ardent member of the fraternity up to the time of his death in 1919.

Master Mason TR, visiting the Scottish Rite Temple in Little Rock, Arkansas, obviously enjoys the fraternity's open platform. His celebrity lent new legitimacy and openness to an institution long distrusted for its alleged secrecy.

Roosevelt's unabashed pride in the brotherhood reflected its restored stature: the most famous Freemason of the new twentieth century was one of us.

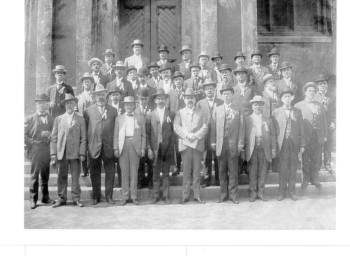

150

Grand Commander Richardson and Grand General Secretary Cowles at an international Masonic conference in Washington in 1912. Albert Pike would have approved; although he never attended or hosted an international meeting, Pike promoted the concept.

Richardson died just as the new House of the Temple opened, and in 1914 George Fleming Moore became the thirteenth Grand Commander of the Supreme Council. In his tenure, which spanned the World War and ended in resignation three years after the Armistice, Moore shared the stage with General Secretary John Henry Cowles, a fraternal collaboration viewed by some historians as a kind of shadow dance to define the soul and future of the Scottish Rite.

At Niagara Falls in 1917, halfway through the honeymoon, Moore and Cowles betray no evidence of strain over the coming shift of power.

Prior to becoming General Secretary, Cowles (front row, fourth from left) was president of the Masonic Relief Association of the United States and Canada, 1907–09.

Grand Commander
Moore poses dutifully
with members' wives at
a visit to a country lodge.

153

John Cowles in the office of the *Masonic Home Journal*, which he edited in 1911. This was the beginning of a lifelong commitment to Masonic publishing, which continued in his enthusiasm for the Scottish Rite's *The New Age Magazine*, founded earlier in 1904.

George Fleming Moore, an Alabaman, was thirteenth Grand Commander of the Supreme Council of the Scottish Rite from 1914 to 1921.

Moore's tenure tested the boundaries of what the fraternity could or could not become, an institutional conflict which paralleled a similar process taking place in American society. From 1904 until his ascendancy, Moore was the first editor of *The New Age Magazine* (later *Scottish Rite Journal*),

the official publication of the Southern Jurisdiction. His writing advocated a form of "Americanism" that was often anti-Catholic and anti-immigration. In his new role as leader, he attempted to combine the main strengths of the two giants preceding him, one an institution builder and the other a values builder. It soon became apparent that he had seriously misread both Pike's and Richardson's legacies.

ALEX.-WASHN. LODGE #22 A.F.+A.M.
ALEXANDRIA, VA.

President Taft with George Washington's apron, jewel, and trowel. Taft expressed a desire to become a Freemason a year before his candidacy and was made a member "at sight" in Cincinnati in early 1909. "I am glad to be here, and to be a Mason," he said. "Many years ago, my father stood in the same place and expressed his love and admiration of the order."

At the laying of the cornerstone of the Alexandria memorial in 1923, where he was assisted by President Coolidge in spreading the cement with the silver trowel President Washington had used on the cornerstone of the U.S. Capitol, Taft said, "Masonry aims at the promotion of morality and higher living by the cultivation of the social side of man, the rousing in him of the instincts of charity and the foundation of the brotherhood of man and the fatherhood of God."

PHOTO BY
CAUFIELD
AND SHOOK

157

A popular past Grand Master of the Grand Lodge in his native Kentucky, John Henry Cowles received a hero's send-off from Louisville on January 30, 1912, the eve of his move to Washington as General Secretary of the Scottish Rite.

Cowles's vision was different from Moore's, and he was a better administrator. He proved far more adept at keeping his feet under himself in managing the process of dynamic change.

COLISEUM-IN·DPLS.   ANCIENT ACCE
GOLDEN J

D SCOTTISH RITE
EE BANQUET.   MAY 19·1915.

© 1915
BRETZMAN
INDIANAPOLIS, IND.

Facing forward.
Scottish Rite banquet,
Indianapolis, May 17,
1915, celebrating the
centennial of the
Northern Masonic
Jurisdiction. When the
Northern Masonic
Jurisdiction was estab-
lished in 1815, many
of the essential rituals
were provided by its
Southern parent.

Subsequently, when the
Southern Jurisdiction
lost its rituals through
fire and other mishap,
the Northerners returned
the favor with copies
of the original materials
that had given them
their start.

German and Belgian Masons share ceremonies in a field lodge during the early part of World War I.

The German conquerors dine with civilian Masons.

In the new vanguard of celebrity Masons at war's end, John J. "Black Jack" Pershing received his Masonic degrees in Nebraska in 1888, subsequently fought in Cuba and the Philippines, chased Pancho Villa across Mexico, and led the American Expeditionary Forces to victory in 1917–18 as general of the army in Europe.

American soldiers in Masonic regalia during the Great War. Following the Armistice, driven by patriotism and a sense of America's new place in the world, Moore prevailed on a reluctant Supreme Council to underwrite a new outreach for relief of ravaged Europe. The program attempted to export a commitment to philanthropy which the Scottish Rite had not yet embraced at home.

Masonic overseas mission. Grand Commander Moore's outreach abroad program included a Masonic Center in Paris for soldiers in the American Expeditionary Forces. Partly because the concept was in competition with such established and successful relief agencies as the American Red Cross and the American Friends Service Committee, it proved to be a costly failure.

Moore miscalculated on the domestic front as well. In the Red Scare of 1919, terms like "Anglo-Saxon" and "Protestant" became a popular means of defining—and stratifying—American culture. Both at home and abroad, Moore's policies appeared to redefine patriotism and the flag as exclusive. In an organization whose founding leadership was almost equally divided among Protestants, Catholics, and Jews, this approach was seriously at odds with Scottish Rite history and tradition.

161

163

In commemoration of the Great War, Cowles lays a wreath at the Tomb of the Unknown Soldier.

While Moore traveled around the country and abroad, General Secretary Cowles often remained in Washington where he was de facto head of Scottish Rite operations. He was in an ideal position to assist the Supreme Council in working through to a diplomatic, humane resolution of a serious crisis in the Scottish Rite's identity. George Fleming Moore's departure was accomplished quietly and without open rancor or scandal, the public largely unaware that it was a forced resignation.

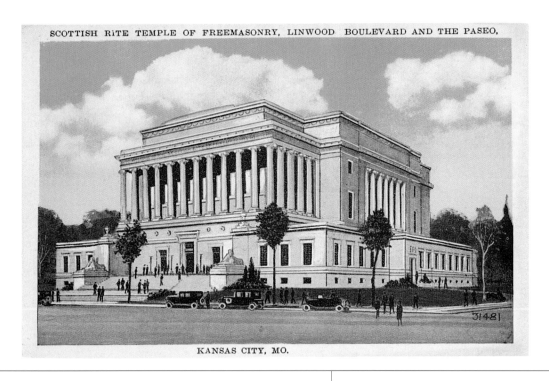

SCOTTISH RITE TEMPLE OF FREEMASONRY, LINWOOD BOULEVARD AND THE PASEO,

31481

KANSAS CITY, MO.

164

The Masonic movement expanded with a growing country, a stabilizing anchor to America's midcentury claims of sovereignty from sea to shining sea. Likewise, the architecture of the Scottish Rite's meeting places evolved as an expression of the fraternity's changing role in the lives of its members and in the larger world.

In the beginning, lodges typically met in the rented upstairs room of a tavern, a natural social center of colonial and postrevolutionary American culture.

Lodges graduated from taverns to freestanding halls in the first half of the nineteenth century, usually with commercial space at street level and the meeting room above.

The turn into the twentieth century was marked by expressions of America's newfound exuberance, wealth, and confidence.

Pictured on these pages, from left to right, are the Scottish Rite Temple of Kansas City, Missouri; the Scottish Rite Cathedral, Indianapolis, Indiana; and the Scottish Rite Temple of Baltimore, Maryland, also designed by John Russell Pope.

43:—SCOTTISH RITE TEMPLE OF FREE MASONRY, BALTIMORE, MD.

48496

This cornerstone ceremony for a new bank in the 1920s is at the site in Charleston, South Carolina, originally occupied by Shepheard's Tavern, birthplace of the Scottish Rite.

With support from the huge membership, the fantastic spaces of the imagination in Pike's era became a reality. The Masonic building boom that began with the House of the Temple continued in the construction of magnificent Scottish Rite meeting places across the United States.

The buildings included auditoriums on the scale of the grandest opera houses. The Scottish Rite embraced the new technology of the visual and performing arts, producing dazzling effects with creative uses of filtered lights and painted backdrops, and adapting the medium of the theater in support of its pageantry and ritual.

Success begets success, and with the rise of heroic architecture, the growth rate of membership in the Scottish Rite achieved unprecedented levels.

Pictured on these pages, from left to right, are Scottish Rite Temples in Pasadena, California; McAllister, Oklahoma; Oakland, California; Guthrie, Oklahoma; and San Antonio, Texas.

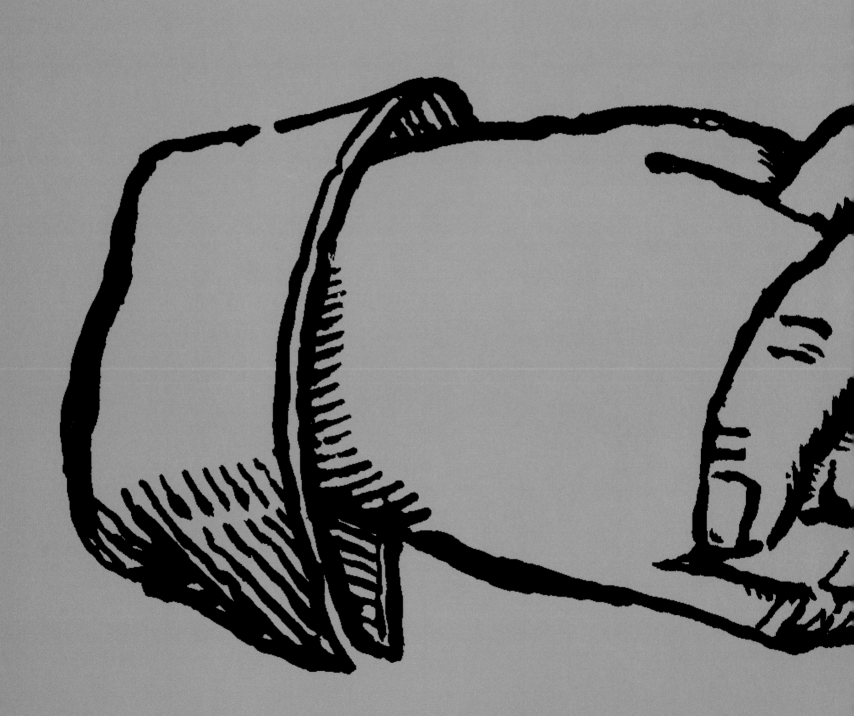

HOLDING THE CENTER

From Cowles to Kleinknecht

GRAND COMMANDER COWLES

commenced his long stewardship at the start of the Roaring Twenties, when both the Scottish Rite and the United States were buoyed up on a rising wave of unparalleled vigor, optimism, and prosperity. In that decade a young St. Louis Mason named Charles Lindbergh made the first solo crossing of the Atlantic by air, while in the opposite direction a torrent of illegal alcohol flowed across the dry nation's borders to fuel what appears to have been a nonstop party. The stock market reached new highs as well, along with membership in the Scottish Rite. ☞ But on Black Friday, October 29, 1929, the wave broke. With the world's economy in collapse, the color of the future darkened. ☞ Nazism, Fascism, and Socialism all gained new life amidst the financial and social ruins of Europe, as in this country one in every four Americans was without a job. By the end of the 1930s, the nascent European war threatened to involve America; by the end of 1941 it embraced more than half the world. After a hard-won victory, America was committed to a massive humanitarian rebuilding of its vanquished enemies. But international hostilities darkened the horizon for four more decades, starting with the Korean conflict and the long Cold War. With skill and vision John Cowles guided the Scottish Rite through the storms and shoals of history, from the heights

of 1920s optimism through the depths
of the Great Depression and the chaos
of a world at war, for a total of thirty-
two years. He was succeeded in 1952
by a self-effacing North Carolina
lawyer and banker, Thomas Harkins,
who three years later was followed as
Grand Commander by Mississippi
attorney Luther A. Smith. ☞ In
1969, the mantle fell to Henry Clausen,
a Californian born on the eve of the
great San Francisco earthquake and
destined, in his own words, "to sur-

vive calamitous events." After a sixteen-year tenure distinguished by the promotion of membership growth and services, the modernizing of rituals, and his advocacy of Scottish Rite centers for learning-disabled children, Clausen was succeeded by the present Grand Commander, C. Fred Kleinknecht. The center has held. The tradition of self-renewal is intact. The Scottish Rite prepares for the coming new millennium.

In 1921, John Cowles leads a delegation of Italian Freemasons in a pilgrimage to Mount Vernon. The group includes Grand Commander, Northern Jurisdiction, Leon Abbott and Grand Commander, Italy, Raoul V. Palermi.

175

On the White House lawn, Cowles introduces his Italian visitors to vice president Calvin Coolidge. Although he was not a Mason, Coolidge's wife Grace was a member of the Order of the Eastern Star, and his son, John, became a Master Mason near the end of World War II. "It has not been my fortune to know very much of Freemasonry," Coolidge had told the Grand Lodge of Massachusetts some years earlier, "but I have had the great fortune to know many Freemasons, and I have been able in that way to judge the tree by its fruits. I know of your high ideals. I have seen that you hold your meetings in the presence of the open Bible, and I know that men who observe that formality have high sentiments of citizenship, of worth, and of character."

By the early twentieth century more than 6,000,000 Americans belonged to "secret societies," all based on the Masonic model of ritual degrees and frequently aided by dramatic ceremonials. These popular social institutions drew on the sophistication of stagecraft, consciously competing with legitimate theater for the growing leisure time of America's middle class.

Charles S. Lobingier (front row, center), Masonic author and founder of the Scottish Rite in the Philippines and China, with a degree team. Combining Pike's revised rituals with the flash and color of vaudeville and grand opera, these teams were responsible for dramatic aspects in the bestowal of Scottish Rite degrees.

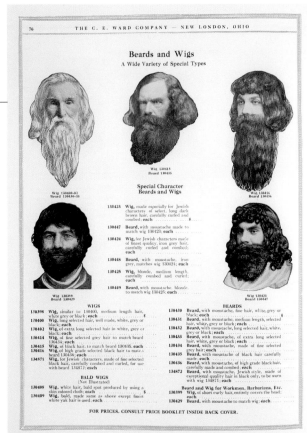

The growing theatricality
of Masonic ritual created
a minor industry. Regalia
catalogs offered hundreds
of stage items, including
masks, hoodwinks, wigs,
beards, costumes, fur-
nishings, props, and
other artifacts.

Theater backdrops enlivened and romanticized the ancient Masonic legacy and its legends. Above: Sosman and Landis, Quarry near Gath, 10th Degree, circa 1905. Left: Great Western Stage, Court of the Dead, 31st Degree, circa 1920s. Right: Sosman and Landis Scene, Peristyle, 18th Degree, circa 1905.

This fraternity group
from Connecticut wears
costuming and makeup
typical of casts in silent
movie features from
the American frontier or
The Arabian Nights.

Regalia worn by this degree team reveals how working Americans could cast off twentieth-century concerns, along with twentieth-century clothing, and transport themselves into the mythic realm of ritual. Here bankers, stockbrokers, schoolteachers, and politicians transform themselves into high priests, kings, guards, and ancient craftsmen.

182

From the outside, this lodge in Stockton, California, looks more like a furniture store than a temple, similar in concept if not in scale to the earlier Masonic meeting halls in the upper rooms of taverns and other commercial establishments. The interior scenes (at right) reveal the true nature of the sanctum sanctorum.

Scottish Rite Temple, Mobile, Alabama, in 1924. The heroic entrances, the sloping, siege-resistant walls, and the archer's windows suggest a ziggurat, a terraced pyramid of Assyrian or Babylonian design, or an ancient fortress. Similarly exotic styles of architecture were gaining favor with builders of the new movie theaters springing up across the country, often with such Masonic-sounding names as Bijou (jewel), Orpheum (after the author of the Orphic mysteries), or Palace. Whether in temple or movie palace, the architecture both protected and advertised the mysteries within.

183

Masonic luminaries stand inside the massive light fixture that will dominate the five-story auditorium of the Davenport Masonic Temple, nearing completion in Iowa.

The finished auditorium, Davenport, Iowa.

The pipe organ began its career as a secular instrument, popular in stadiums, music halls, and public drinking places before it gained acceptance in houses of worship. No doubt the appeal of a pipe organ in the Masonic temple was the solemnity it lent to ritual and other theatrical productions, and its association by then in the public mind with religious ceremony. This pipe organ in the Davenport Temple is big enough to seat a small banquet.

President Harding meets on the White House lawn with members of the National Sojourners, a Masonic organization of former military officers that includes John Cowles (beside Marine officer in white uniform at right), then Grand Commander of the Scottish Rite.

Warren Harding was initiated in Marion, Ohio, in 1901, but was not passed and raised until August 1920, the same year he resigned his senate seat and was nominated as the Republican candidate for the presidency. A year later, President Harding addressed the National League of Masonic Clubs in Washington. "No man ever took the oaths and subscribed to the obligations with a greater watchfulness and care than I have exercised in receiving the various rites of Masonry, and I say with due deliberation and without fear of breaking faith, I have never encountered a lesson, never witnessed an example, never heard an obligation uttered which could not be proclaimed to the world."

Harding remained a loyal Mason to the end. On the day of his death on August 2, 1923, he chose a Masonic audience in Hollywood, California, to receive his last message (delivered by his secretary) to the American people.

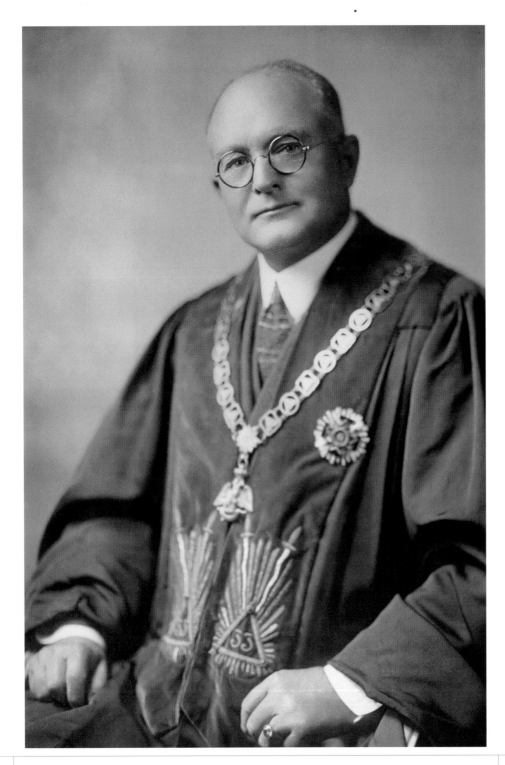

Cowles as Grand Commander. John H. Cowles was an officer in his Kentucky regiment in the Spanish-American War, became a Scottish Rite Mason in Puerto Rico, and for the rest of his life preferred being addressed as Captain Cowles. Not as proactive as Pike, Richardson, or Moore, Cowles' particular strength was an ability to understand and adapt to changing times. He lived in an apartment in the House of the Temple and knew everybody in Washington, including J. Edgar Hoover, members of Congress, and the foreign diplomatic corps.

Previously the head of a Louisville brass foundry, in his leadership of the Scottish Rite he saw himself as a businessman who had to balance the books at the end of the day, collect the dues, make sure the mortgages were adequately capitalized, and supervise the Scottish Rite's 1920s building boom.

Here Cowles wears Albert Pike's jewel, which Grand Commander Richardson had worn on many formal occasions.

One of many Cowles recordings.

Master of the new media, Cowles speaks over the radio at Council Bluffs, Iowa, in the 1920s. At that same time, he used "phonographic educa-tion" to carry the story of the Scottish Rite—and his voice—to the far-flung membership. Also an ardent fan of cinema, he wrote, "It has been my custom to go to the pictures about five nights a week. After an early dinner, I take in the pic-tures then return to my office to work."

The George Washington Masonic National Memorial in Alexandria, Virginia, is a facsimile of the Pharos lighthouse on the shores of Alexandria in ancient Egypt. Built after the House of the Temple, this ambitious construction project could never have been completed without the financial contributions and enthusiasm of the leadership of the Scottish Rite. Cowles, who was in on the project from its beginning, is shown here (in back row, with derby, just to right of left-most column) with Memorial Association members at an early planning session at Mount Vernon in 1911.

The cornerstone and the memorial under construction in the 1920s.

Cowles at a meeting
of the Northern and
Southern Jurisdictions
in Boston, with Scottish
Rite leaders from New
Jersey.

As Grand Commander,
Cowles traveled thou-
sands of miles every year
and began to build rela-
tionships with Scottish
Rite counterparts in
Europe, Asia, and Latin
America. Here he disem-
barks at Liverpool with
a Scottish Rite delegation
of the Southern and
Northern Jurisdictions
on its way to an interna-
tional conference at
Lausanne, Switzerland,
in 1922.

Cowles at Lahneck
Lodge, Scotland, in 1922.
Scotland was the mythi-
cal birthplace of the
Scottish Rite.

Cowles exiting an airplane in Romania, 1926. In the year before Lindbergh's Atlantic conquest, commercial aviation was still in its infancy, an adventure for the privileged few.

Cowles in Bucharest lodge, 1926.

At attention on the steps of the Erectheum of the Acropolis, Athens, 1926.

With companions under the canopy of the rain forest in Panama, 1926, and in another jungle setting, with fellow Masons, on a Cowles trip to Rio de Janeiro.

In Egypt, the fez was still as commonplace as the bowler in Britain or the fedora Cowles now wore in America.

Cowles stands with Dr. Wang Chung Hui, a Chinese Mason, also a member of a secret Tong society, whose freedom he negotiated following an incident in Tientsin.

The Masonic touring party was leaving the city of Tientsin when a column of troops of the Chihli-Shantung army cut across the route of their slow-moving motorcade and one of the soldiers was accidentally knocked down by the car carrying Cowles. Although the foreign visitors were all allowed to continue on, the only Chinese occupant, a brother Mason, was detained for five hours by the military police. Tientsin, near Beijing, had been the site of severe fighting and the famous siege during the Boxer uprising in 1900, less than three decades earlier. Because Cowles realized that under martial law the Chinese national was at serious risk, he refused to leave without him. Newspapers picked up the story, inaccurately describing Cowles and his party (above, top) as "under house arrest" during their wait for their companion to be freed.

The peripatetic leader
voyages on.

Cowles with degree
team, Wichita, Kansas.
A bachelor, Cowles
felt his real family
was his Scottish Rite
brotherhood.

The Kansas City (Missouri) Temple of the Scottish Rite. The design is a visual echo of the John Russell Pope masterpiece in Washington, D.C.

Cowles with Kansas City Scottish Rite leaders.

Inside, Cowles performs with a group onstage.

A full house, typical of the turnouts for a visit by the Grand Commander.

Perhaps the planet's most famous living person at the time of this photograph, Charles Lindbergh (to right of speaker) is honored by a lodge in Panama in the 1930s. The "Lone Eagle" received his degrees in St. Louis in 1926, the year before his nonstop solo flight from New York to Paris raised him from obscurity and electrified the world. During that historic thirty-eight-hour trip, he wore the square and compass on the lapel of his flight jacket as a charm, the revelation of which gave rise to his other nickname, "Lucky Lindy." Lindbergh's visit to Panama was probably related to his new career with Pan American Airways. His survey flights, generally in float planes or larger Sikorsky flying boats, led to the opening of commercial air routes throughout Latin America, around the Pacific Rim, and eventually across the Atlantic.

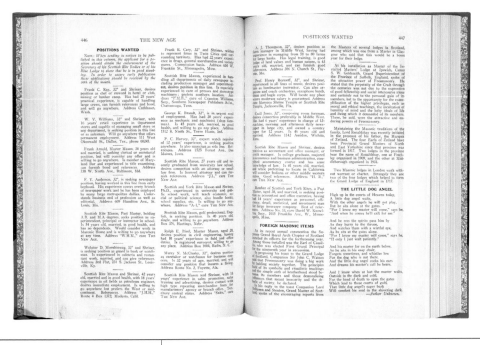

The new hard times of the Great Depression are reflected in these "Positions Wanted" ads from *The New Age Magazine,* part of Cowles' efforts to establish a Scottish Rite job placement service. He also developed a reputation for his quiet personal generosity, rarely failing to respond to any legitimate request for help from a needy Mason or his family.

Franklin Delano Roosevelt received his Masonic degrees in 1911 in New York City, while serving in the state senate. During his later years in the White House, at the time of this photograph, he confided his admiration for the 33rd Degree.

FDR was a member of the Northern Jurisdiction, where Cowles' counterpart, Melvin Johnson, encountered resistance from two members of his Supreme Council who considered FDR a traitor to his class and opposed giving him the 33rd Degree. So Johnson proposed to Cowles that in the interest of Masonic harmony the degree be granted instead in Washington, by Cowles, under special dispensation.

In a "personal and confidential" letter of October 6, 1943, Cowles replied that he was "very fond of a goodly number" of the members of the Supreme Council, Northern Masonic Jurisdiction, and that he had always "tried and will continue to try to keep the best fraternal feelings…" For these reasons, he declined Johnson's proposal. Several months later, FDR died without ever receiving the 33rd Degree.

Cowles addresses his constituency in 1940, while America debated possible entry into what was still being called the European War. Cowles was an early proponent of America's entry into the war and took his case to the airwaves.

Friedrich Haſſelbacher

Das Todesurteil über die Freimaurerei in Deutſchland

The Masonic compasses, an inverted pentagram (often associated with the occult or possibly the "Blazing Star" of Freemasonry), and the Jesuit cross all combine to obscure the rising sun of Nazism, "the death sentence over Free-masonry in Germany," in 1935.

The Washington Daily News

Today 9:45 84
Yesterday Highest ..92 Lowest ...71

Served by Four Trunk Wires of United Press—World's Greatest Evening Press Association

14th Year —No. 229   2 Cents   WASHINGTON, D. C., THURSDAY, AUGUST 1, 1935   Entered as Second Class Matter at the Washington, D. C., Post Office

Forecast Partly cloudy, possible local showers tonight and tomorrow; not much change in temperature.

NOON EDITION

NAZIS MOVE AGAINST MASONS

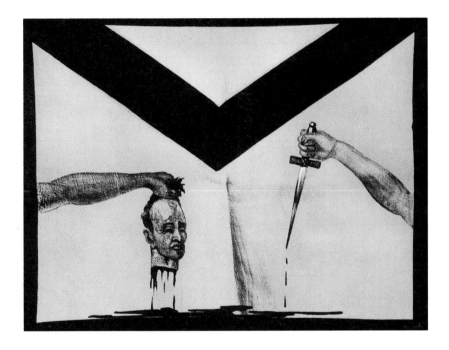

Hitler had already declared war on Free-masonry, ordering the dissolution of all German lodges in late 1934 and proclaiming Masons enemies of the state the following year.

Another poster distorts the meaning of a 9th Degree apron by falsely linking Masonic ritual to human sacrifice. A sharp irony exists in this example of Nazi propaganda because the German Scottish Rite ritual actually interprets its 9th Degree regalia as a reminder that acts of ignorance and errors of judgement always have future consequences.

This German postcard of the 1930s links Masonry to the popular anti-Semitic theme of responsibility in the death of Christ.

206

Jewish and Masonic items are heaped together for a Nazi bonfire; a wave of such incidents culminated in 1938 in the infamous *Kristallnacht*.

Visiting dignitaries at an anti-Masonic exhibit, assembled from looted lodges in increasingly militant Germany. The taller of the two, Arthur Seyss-Inquart, led the Nazi program for the extermination of Dutch Jews. After a trial at Nurenburg, he was hanged on October 16, 1946.

Cowles did not stand mute in the face of Nazi persecution. *The New Age Magazine* had a running update on what was happening to Masons and Jews in Europe. In the 1930s, he personally interceded on behalf of the Grand Commander of the Scottish Rite in Germany, a Jew named Leo Musselman, who later credited Cowles with saving his life.

In the midst of the war, Cowles' 1943 day-book schedules an emergency meeting on Nazi atrocities. It is also true that the term "Holocaust" makes one of its earliest appearances in print in *The New Age Magazine*.

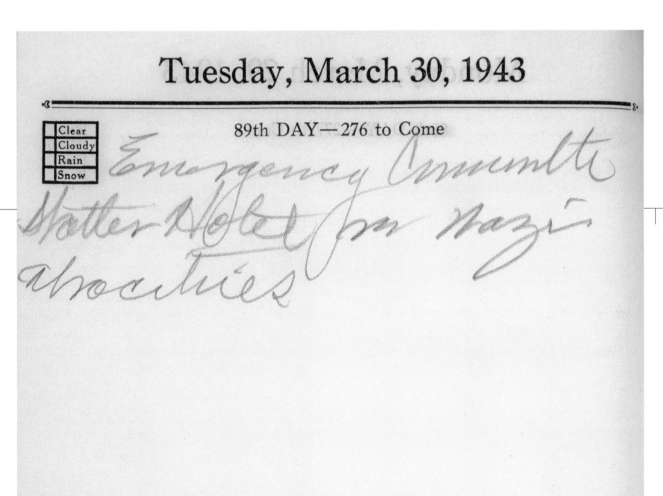

Tuesday, March 30, 1943

☐ Clear
☐ Cloudy
☐ Rain
☐ Snow

89th DAY—276 to Come

Emergency Committee
Statler Hotel for Nazi
atrocities

207

The Masonic Lodge in
Oslo was ransacked
by Nazis shortly after
the start of the German
takeover of Norway and
became an office for
the occupying army.
During and after the war
the Supreme Council,
Southern Jurisdiction,
allocated millions in
food and financial aid
to relieve suffering and
rebuild postwar Europe.

208

American entry into the war carried the Masonic experience to the farthest corners of the world. The battle for Guadalcanal was a turning point in the campaign in the Pacific. The Square and Compass Club met in this open-ended Quonset hut, not behind the lines but in the war zone, in 1943.

Guadalcanal lodge membership card.

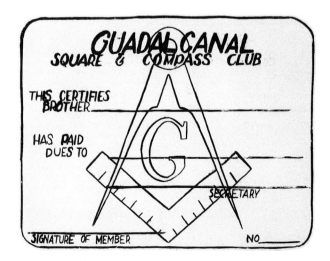

Although membership in lodges in combat areas was restricted by circumstance to Allied servicemen, the war revitalized indigenous Masonic clubs throughout the Pacific. With peace, the Scottish Rite served as a powerful medium in the integration of dissimilar cultures in a new unity of purpose. This membership roster from the Guadalcanal lodge, with names from all over the world, reflects that diversity.

No.	Name	Lodge	Location	Service
705	Ragman Hyne	Lodge Rewa of Vita	Island of Fiji	Resident Civilian Con. Staff
706	Robert H. Holzwarth	Lodge Seneca #920	Rochester N.Y.	221 M.P. Co. USS. PSM 2 USN.
707	Ralph W. Raasch	Wisconsin #13	Milwaukee Wisc.	2- Special US MCB.
708	Lee Roy Blocker	Deerfield #432	Deerfield Kansas	
709	Rex Seavey	Plattsburg #828	Plattsburg N.Y.	923 ABS. Bn
710	Gordon L. Claasen	Service 237	Dunedin New Zealand	RNZAF
711	G.B. Duke	Te Mata #298	Hawkes Bay New Zealand	RNZAF
712	Maurice V. Clark	Humane #21	Rochester N.H.	5 Command 9 Command
713	Horace J. Barnes	Galbright #33	Oxford Miss.	9th STN. Hosp.
714	William H. Jackman	Prineville #76	Prineville Oregon	5 Island & Command
715	Felix H. Morrison	46 C.B. Sq. & Comp. Club (547.)		navy aviation Supp
716	B.L. Jones	Star #187	Cuyahoga Falls Ohio	HQ Sqdn 13 an 7 area
717	D.W. Tagtmeyer	46. C.B.		aviation Supp
~~718~~	~~Howard Mercer~~	~~1394 Engr.~~	~~Jersey Shore Pa.~~	
718	P.A. Malone	Crane 1262	Crane Texas.	34 C.B.
719	Floyd J. Sisson	Regan 1037	Houston Texas	34 C.B.
720	Claude J. Enright	Amuri 184	Nth. Canterbury N.Z.	YMCA RNZAF
721	Kenneth Sexlander	Whatcom 151	Bellingham Wash.	CMB. S.S.
722	Howry. H. Warner	Altadena 678	alt. Calif.	FEA Service
723	Wm. Willis Dobbins	Lagrange 379	Lagrange Ohio	64 Troop carrier Sqd
724	Stewart J. Smith	Dee Guard 278	Farwell Indiana	" "
725	Mallory E. Phillips	Biscayne Bay 1053	Miami Fla.	16 Base P.O. officer APO 709
726	John E. Wicken	Trinidad 284	Trinidad Colo.	Postal official APO 2947
727	Glenn P. Seabold	Sol. D. Bayless 359	Fort Wayne Indiana	905 Sig Coy
728	Thomas Chalklen	Belta Waikato 12	Hamilton New Zealand	RNZAF
729	Selwyn C. Cole	Ohakea Air Force 307	Ohakea New Zealand	"
730	Walter Whishaw	King Hiram 1351	Scottish Palestine	"
731	Lyle A. Welch	Craftsman 314	Lincoln Nebr.	HQ Service Co
732	Joseph C. Sonneborn	Moriah 958	Utica New York	1008th Sig Co
733	Norman E. Watkins	Craftsman 559	Los Angeles Calif.	735th Heavy Shop Co
734	Lynn D. Servaty	J.H. Knapp 238	Knapp Wisconsin	2nd Sp. USNCB
735	David N. Cohen	Moses Michall Hays	Boston Mass.	58th ORD Co.
736	George A. Thele	Progress 657	St. Louis Mo.	Hq. Co. SORS. Comd.
737	Verle E. Wills	Negaunee 202	Negaunee Mich.	39sta Hosp
738	J.E. Webster	Lynwood 600	Lynwood Calif	260th Civil Railroad Co.
739	Chris Lennox	Whetu Kairang	Seatoun N.Z.	RNZAF
740	Alan Lindberg			
741	Vernan L. Paulson	Ark Lodge 126		
742	Lorenz Winterland	Chinoa 292		
743	George W. Nosfell Jr.	Geo. Washington 24	Ogden, Utah	
744	B. Howard Smith	Ivanhoe 446	Kansas City, Mo.	
745	Oliver A. Nation	Siloam 276	Oklahoma City, Okla.	
746	Chauncey W. Farr	Titusville 754	Titusville, Pa.	
747	Kenneth Loraca	Star of Hope 430	Brooklyn, N.Y.	
748	Nemesio Quiton	Apote 29	Philippine Islands	
749	Blake Lowern	Akaton 354	Graham	
750	Richard Cox	Union 2	Madison, Ind.	
751	Henry W. Dobbe	Coconut Grove 258	Miami Florida	
752	Harry Edwards	First Temple 302	Oakland, N.Z.	
753	John W. Ellsworth	Kelly 1131	So. San Antonio, Texas	
754	Ray J. Hennigh	Darrouzett Lodge 1156	Darrouzett, Texas	
755	Roy J. Bruce	Trion Lodge 160	Trion, Georgia	
756	Charles S. Hearty	Rob Morris 92	Denver, Colorado	
757	Donald W. Angell	Crescent 25	Cedar Rapids, Iowa	
758	Elmer J. Keller	Corinthian Temple 805	Rochester, N.Y.	
759	Manuel Garcia	Universal 178	Tampa, Florida	
760	Robert Lewis Heslip	Intermont 269	Narrows, Va.	
761	F.E. De Caroeto	Battleboro 102	Battleboro, Vt.	
762	Robert W. Lloyd	Streaton 607	Streaton, Ill.	
763	Archie L. Holterman	Onaga 188	Onaga, Kansas	
764	G.E. Hassall	Koraarecka 304	Bay of Islands N.Z.	
765	Floyd H. Failer	Warpole 176	Upper Sandusky Ohio	
766	Cyril Shaw	St. Andrew 432	S.C. Dunedin. N.Z.	
767	Stanley C. Samuel	Tutanekai Green 156	Wellington N.Z.	
768	John W. Mitchell	Victory 40	Nelson, N.Z.	
769	Fredrick E. Horn	Ancient Landmark 200	Olin, Iowa	
770	Ira A. Rohrenz Horn	Idaho #1	Boise Idaho	
771	C.R. Rule	Eddy #71	Carlsbad, N.M.	
772	John F. Baskett	Aurora 156	Aurora, Colorado	
773	Merran G. Hill	First Temple 16	Cheshire, Conn.	
774	John D. Robinson	King David	Taunton, Mass.	
775	Kenneth Bentz	Frontier 48	Stillwater, Oklahoma	
776	S.F. Sanders	Atlanta 463	Atlanta, Texas	
777	H.N. Jones	Aransas 1018	Aransas Pass, Texas	
778	Carl R. Anson	Santa Cruz 38	Santa Cruz, Calif.	
779	Clyde H. Armstrong	Milnor 287	Pittsburgh, Pa.	
780	Roy Lockhart	Newcastle 494	New Castle, Indiana	
781	Walter B. Wallace	Southland 273	Southland, N.Z.	
782	N.T.R. Joynt	St. Geo. #79	Temuka N.Z.	
783	Alex J. Baxter	Pt. Chevalier 303	Auckland N.Z.	

D E F G H I J K L M N O P Q R S T U V W X Y Z

Scottish Rite bond rallies raised millions for the war effort. Often, the symbolic goal of these drives was a specific ship or aircraft—in this case, a giant Martin flying boat. This type of aircraft was favored for long flights over water because it could land if faced with mechanical problems—but also

because, prior to the war, there were no paved airports in the Pacific capable of supporting the weight of long-distance passenger and cargo aircraft. The plaque installed on this behemoth by the Bureau of Aeronautics reads, "The Philippine Mars, sponsored and made possible by War Bond purchases of the Supreme Council (Mother Council of the

World) of the Thirty Third Degree, Ancient and Accepted Scottish Rite of Free Masonry, Southern Jurisdiction, USA. Presented October 15, 1945." Grand Commander Cowles, center, presided at the dedication ceremony.

Already enrolled at Benjamin Franklin University, future Grand Commander C. Fred Kleinknecht (left) joined the navy, becoming an aviation machinist mate, first class, shortly after America joined the war.

In one of the most famous photographs of World War II, General Douglas MacArthur delivers on his promise to the Philippine people, "I shall return," wading ashore in the van of his liberating army.

Less than a decade later, when MacArthur flew to his mid-Pacific rendezvous with President Truman during the Korean War, he made one of his few strategic errors, timing his arrival to make it appear that his commander-in-chief had to come to him, rather than the other way around. Cowles could have told him it wouldn't work. Like Truman, the Old Soldier was a 33rd Degree Mason.

PEARL HARBOR ATTACK

HEARINGS

BEFORE THE

JOINT COMMITTEE ON THE INVESTIGATION OF THE PEARL HARBOR ATTACK

CONGRESS OF THE UNITED STATES

SEVENTY-NINTH CONGRESS

FIRST SESSION

PURSUANT TO

S. Con. Res. 27

A CONCURRENT RESOLUTION AUTHORIZING AN
INVESTIGATION OF THE ATTACK ON PEARL
HARBOR ON DECEMBER 7, 1941, AND
EVENTS AND CIRCUMSTANCES
RELATING THERETO

PART 35

CLAUSEN INVESTIGATION

Printed for the use of the
Joint Committee on the Investigation of the Pearl Harbor Attack

UNITED STATES
GOVERNMENT PRINTING OFFICE
WASHINGTON : 1946

78716

In 1944, future Grand Commander Henry C. Clausen was asked by War Secretary Henry L. Stimson to reinvestigate the Japanese attack on Pearl Harbor. Clausen's report was based on 55,000 miles of travel and over 100 interviews around the world.

In testifying before Congress, Clausen blamed the surprise of Pearl Harbor on poor communication, ending unfounded rumors that either FDR or George Marshall knew of the attack in advance and permitted it for political reasons.

HIGHHOLD
HUNTINGTON, LONG ISLAND

November 15, 1946.

Hon. Robert P. Patterson,
The Secretary of War,
Washington, D. C.

Dear Judge Patterson:

I have been concerned over the fact that
the Decorations and Awards Board has not recognized
by suitable decoration the distinguished services
of Lieutenant Colonel Henry C. Clausen whose thorough
and able analysis of the evidence given before the
Army Pearl Harbor Board and his later investigation
of additional evidence, including the interviewing
of officers in all parts of the world, was of such
outstanding value.

I consider that Colonel Clausen carried
out his great responsibilities, which were of such
importance that they might well have been assigned
to a General Officer of the Army, with judicial fair-
ness, with dignity, and with great professional skill.
I hope that it will be possible for the Decorations
and Awards Board to review the record to determine
whether a decoration would not be an appropriate
recognition of his services.

Very sincerely yours,

Henry L Stimson

By the late 1940s, ideological seeds sewn by the Masonic presence in the war had blossomed throughout Asia and the Pacific. This Masonic temple is in Japan.

Interior of Masonic temple in Japan.

This Scottish Rite temple in Manila was restored to its original use after being nearly destroyed during the Japanese occupation.

Dedication of the flagpole
in front of the Scottish
Rite Temple in Balboa,
Panama Canal Zone,
a gift of the Franklin
Delano Roosevelt Class
of 1945.

Scottish Rite lodge in
Honolulu.

215

Harry Truman, who succeeded to the presidency upon the death of Roosevelt, speaks from the East at a Masonic lodge in Indiana during a whistle stop in the 1948 election. Popularly known as the Man from Missouri, Truman was a former Grand Master of Missouri Masons and a natural choice for the 33rd Degree. Cowles invited the President to the House of the Temple for a courtesy call.

When Truman responded to Cowles's invitation, it became apparent that he saw their relationship in a different light. The man who had made the decision on Hiroshima and Nagasaki, the leader of the Western World, pointedly replied that if Cowles wanted to meet with him, he could come to the White House. Cowles did.

Two years later, this heroic statue of George Washington was erected in a cavernous alcove of the George Washington Masonic National Memorial Temple in Alexandria, Virginia. Truman crossed the river to attend the unveiling ceremony and preside at the dedication.

Faithful to his lifelong Masonic commitment, Truman met with members of the Scottish Rite, including Cowles, again in 1951.

Harvey J. Crown
1951

Merry Christmas and
a Happy New Year

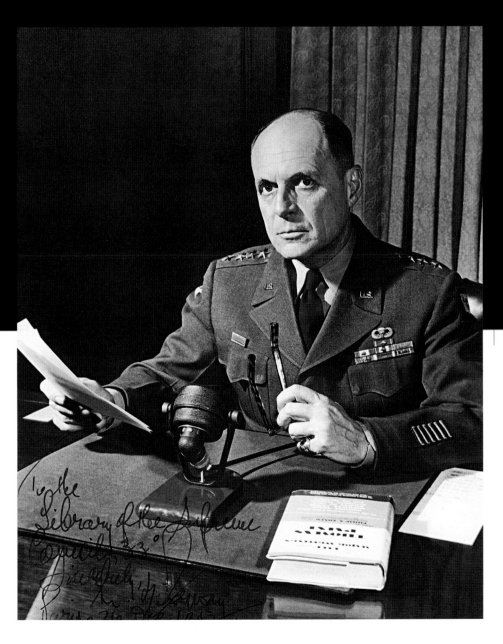

General Matthew Ridgway, who succeeded MacArthur as commander of allied forces in Korea, became a Mason early in his career as a soldier and took it very seriously. When offered the 33rd Degree in the early 1950s, Ridgway refused on the basis of not having earned the honor. Even when the proposal was repeated, he didn't budge.

A wartime Christmas greeting from a Mason in uniform.

AG Section, Hq AFFE/8A
APO 343, San Francisco, Calif.

25 January 1955

Mr. Thomas J. Harkins, 33°
Sovereign Grand Commander
A & A Scottish Rite, S.J.
1733 Sixteenth St., N.W.
Washington, D. C.

Dear Brother Harkins,

When I last wrote, I stated that I would send you some pictures of
the ceremony of presenting the $2,000.00 check for the Pusan Children's
Charity Hospital. I have had some difficulty in obtaining the negatives,
but they are finally available, and I am forwarding the pictures to you.
In addition, I am sending a few pictures which show the Hospital and
some of its patients.

You will be glad to know that we are definitely going to have the
new Hospital building. The support which we have obtained from Masons
and their friends all over the country has been most gratifying.

To insure perpetuation of the project, I am organizing "The Friends
of Pusan Children's Charity Hospital" among former members of the Pusan
Masonic Club and others who may be interested. That way I feel that we
can capitalize on their participation and keep it alive for the future.
Brother Bedillion and Brother Eichorn, Grand Master for the District
Grand Lodge for Japan, have both consented to serve. In view of your
interest in the Hospital, I should very much like to enroll you (with
your permission) as a charter member, and I hope that you will accept
this invitation.

With best regards, I remain,

Sincerely and fraternally,

Roger M. Crosby, 32°
Colonel, U. S. Army

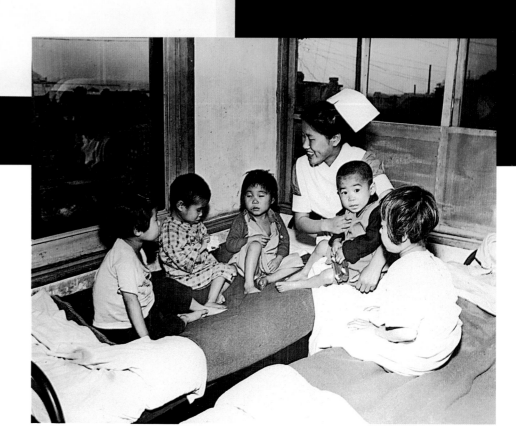

Pusan Children's Charity
Hospital in Korea was
built and supported by
Masonic contributions
from all over the world.

A warm, soft-spoken attorney from Ashville, North Carolina, Thomas J. Harkins was elected to replace John Cowles as Grand Commander in October 1952. The previous February, Cowles apparently tripped on a rug and was hospitalized after the resulting fall. Over the coming months it became apparent that he was incapable of resuming his duties, and after thirty-two years as Grand Commander, he resigned that September.

Harkins, a lifelong Mason, was seventy-three. He resigned just three years later in the face of impending blindness. In his brief tenure, he established the Scottish Rite Foundation and began the first national programs for children with learning and language disabilities.

John Cowles, whose length of service as Grand Commander was second only to Albert Pike's, died in June 1954. His interment had been arranged by Cowles through a special act of Congress.

In Washington, all burials have to be in the ground, and until then the only exceptions were the tombs of Woodrow Wilson and a handful of other statesmen and clergy in the National Cathedral. But in anticipation of his death, Cowles had argued ten years earlier that ancient Masonic custom, going back to Solomon, allows the builder of the temple to be buried inside the place that he built, administered, loved, and cared for.

Accordingly, on October 29, 1944, Albert Pike's remains were exhumed from the Oak Hill Cemetery—where, in accordance with his wishes, his family had left the grave unmarked for twenty-six years— and were interred, with appropriate inscriptions, in the House of the Temple. A decade later, John Cowles was enshrined beside him.

ORDER OF THE RAINBOW FOR GIRLS
GUAM ~ 1955
FOTO BY: JANOC

Luther A. Smith arrives on the mid-Pacific island of Guam shortly after his election as Grand Commander of the Scottish Rite in 1955.

The Order of the Rainbow for Girls was founded as a young women's auxiliary of the Scottish Rite by William Mark Sexson, a minister who was Grand Master of the Grand Lodge in Oklahoma. In 1955, these Rainbow Girls, most of them the wives or daughters of American military personnel, cut a festive cake in honor of Smith's visit.

Raised in a Mississippi Lodge in 1907 and a deeply committed Mason, Luther Smith, sixty-eight, was an attorney and judge of the court of chancery when elected to the highest office of the Scottish Rite.

Smith officiates at a cornerstone ceremony in Guam, part of a two-month tour of the Far East on behalf of the Supreme Council in the spring of 1958. The trip's purpose, Smith told the council, was "to revive our personal association with our brethren in the Orient and to thereby encourage them."

Smith and his wife,
Lorraine, seek shelter
from the equatorial
sun at another Guam
reception.

Gifts and endowments
from the Scottish Rite
supported research and
scholarship, trained
future American leaders
in international law and
diplomacy, and helped
underwrite the new na-
tional priority on higher
education at such leading
institutions as American
University, Baylor, and
Vanderbilt. By 1960, The

George Washington
University had received
nearly $2,000,000, and
President Cloyd H.
Marvin, a 33rd Degree
Scottish Rite Mason,
estimated that a third of
the operating budget of
the School of Government
(above) came from the
Scottish Rite Endowment.

The 1960s were a turning point in the growth of Masonic membership throughout the country. Despite scholarship efforts of the Scottish Rite Fellowship Program, there was a widening generational division between the fathers who had joined during and after the "good" war and the coming wave of baby boomers who were learning to mistrust or ridicule the old institutions. There was a time lag as the Scottish Rite membership process continued to draw from the Blue Lodge reservoir, but the cycle was headed for a downturn.

Dwight Eisenhower, the first military leader elected to the presidency since Ulysses S. Grant, symbolized America's patriotic moral contentment. Although he never became a Mason, he often sounded like one, both in speeches which reflected familiar Masonic values and in his friendly relationship with the fraternity.

Ike spreads the mortar at a Washington cornerstone ceremony for the new wing of the Capitol building on July 1, 1950. Masonic onlookers include Carl Hayden (front row, left), senator from Arizona since 1926, and Senate Majority Leader Everett Dirksen of Illinois (front row, second from right), who received the 33rd Degree in Boston in 1954.

Grand Commander Luther Smith and Hurst Anderson, president of American University, view the foundation of the new School of International Service in 1958. The Scottish Rite also contributed $20,000 to an AU chair in American Studies.

Smith speaks at a
biennial session of the
Supreme Council near
the end of his tenure.

A visiting dignitary bows
to the Council—and per-
haps, symbolically, to
the future. U.S. Secretary
of the Treasury Robert
B. Anderson receives the
Grand Cross in 1959.
Behind him, nearer to
camera, stands future
Grand Commander
Henry C. Clausen.

Temple room during
biennial session with
the Grand Commander
presiding in the tradi-
tional East.

John F. Kennedy won a tight presidential race in 1960 and the following April received these members of the Eighth International Conference of Supreme Councils and their wives at the White House. Kennedy's example had already had a significant impact on preferences in men's headwear—but obviously not on those of Henry C. Clausen, in background at right in dark coat and hat.

The numerical parity of Catholics, Protestants, and Jews in the founding membership of the Scottish Rite had long ago melted away as the country became predominantly Protestant. But while Jewish membership remained fairly steady relative to the population as a whole, for many years the number of Catholics in the Scottish Rite had been negligible.

Although the Scottish Rite fueled the earlier division by its rigorous opposition to the public funding of parochial education, Roman Catholics were never prohibited by Masons from joining; rather, the Church took the position that Catholics couldn't participate in anything they couldn't tell their priest. By the 1960s, however, with membership rules widely published and Masonic practices subject to

honest public scrutiny, the perception of secrecy was on its way to becoming a moot issue. Kennedy's relaxed relationship with the Scottish Rite set the tone for a future modest comeback in Catholic membership.

235

A young C. Fred
Kleinknecht as a staff
member of the Scottish
Rite, on the pathway to
becoming Grand
Commander. In 1963
he accepts an honor
from the Samuel
Gompers Lodge #45 on
behalf of Ray Baker
Harris, librarian of the
Supreme Council.

Grand Commander
Smith bestows the 33rd
Degree on Mercury
astronaut Gordon Cooper
in a capping ceremony
at the Supreme Council
headquarters.

Kleinknecht with astronaut Gordon Cooper.

Smith with Apollo astronaut Buzz Aldrin.

Scottish Rite flag carried to the moon and back by Cooper.

Scottish Rite flag carried on the moon and back by Aldrin.

Kleinknecht welcomes Aldrin as he arrives at the House of the Temple.

NATIONAL AERONAUTICS AND SPACE ADMINISTRATION
MANNED SPACECRAFT CENTER
HOUSTON, TEXAS 77058

IN REPLY REFER TO: September 19, 1969

Illustrious Luther A. Smith, 33°
Sovereign Grand Commander
Supreme Council, 33°
Southern Jurisdiction, U.S.A.
1733 16th Street, N.W.
Washington, D.C. 20009

Dear Grand Commander:

     It was a great moment in my life to be so cordially welcomed
to the House of the Temple on September 16, 1969, by you and Grand
Secretary General Kleinknecht, 33°, and also the members of your
staffs. My greatest pleasure, however, was to be able to present
to you on this occasion the Scottish Rite Flag which I carried on
the Apollo 11 Flight to the Moon--emblazoned in color with the
Scottish Rite Double-headed Eagle, the Blue Lodge Emblem and the
Sovereign Grand Commander's Insignia.

     I take this opportunity to again thank you for the autographed
copy of your recent book, entitled "Action by the Scottish Rite,
Southern Jurisdiction, U.S.A.," which is filled with a wealth of
information about your Americanism Program sponsored by the Supreme
Council, participating activities and related activities of the
Rite.

                              Cordially and fraternally,

                              Edwin E. Aldrin, Jr.
                              NASA Astronaut

When President Kennedy announced his goal of an American on the moon by the end of the 1960s, it's unlikely he imagined there would be two of them—and least of all that they'd both be Scottish Rite Masons.

But it made sense. The Scottish Rite closely identified itself with the victory in space, with the triumph of the positive side of American culture.

In the same way, it once identified with the pioneer spirit of Albert Pike, with the ruggedly indomitable Teddy Roosevelt at San Juan Hill or in the jungles of South America, and with the feisty, down-home integrity of Harry Truman.

But in other ways the space race was different. The ultimate example of American "can-do" boosterism, NASA operated the parallel machinery of nearly unimaginable technological mastery and a program of unrelenting public relations. The moonshot is the best story of the "feel-good" 60s—and one of the best of all time. But its impact on America's spirit was shadowed by turmoil, the "feel-bad" side of that same decade. The technology triumphed, but the PR somehow seemed to miss the mark.

One of the problems was that the Scottish Rite hardly identified with the civil rights movement, the anti-war movement, the War on Poverty, the Great Society, or the other powerful forces that were shaping the evolving national ethos. They didn't oppose those forces, but their focus was on aspirations of a different kind. Space may be the final frontier, but of all the choices, the Scottish Rite focused on the one that was non-populist.

A generation of young Americans saw the fulfillment of Kennedy's vision as a triumph of human intellect, courage, will, and spirit. But there was a parallel sense that in other ways the space race was an artificial model, an organizational triumph without question, but perhaps not a victory of the same magnitude for individualism. Challenges and frontiers had changed with the times. Something seemed to be missing.

Grand Commander
Henry C. Clausen,
formerly the Grand
Inspector General for
California.

Richard Nixon receives a
delegation of Scottish
Rite Masons in the White
House. With the impact
of television, Vietnam,
the automobile, the draft,
a sickening wave of
political assassinations,
an imperial presidency,
Watergate, and the
vaunted loss of the
American hero, the coun-
try was experiencing a
widening gap between
Them and Us.

This growing din of
point and counterpoint
extended well beyond the
nation's leadership and
was far more than a
simple generation gap.
Once again, the challenge
to the Scottish Rite was
the creative realignment
of public perception
with the true character,
energy, and vision of
the fraternity.

240   Clausen speaking at a
        biennial session.

Smith and Clausen at the
National Cathedral. They
stand before the statue of
George Washington that
the Scottish Rite helped
to commission.

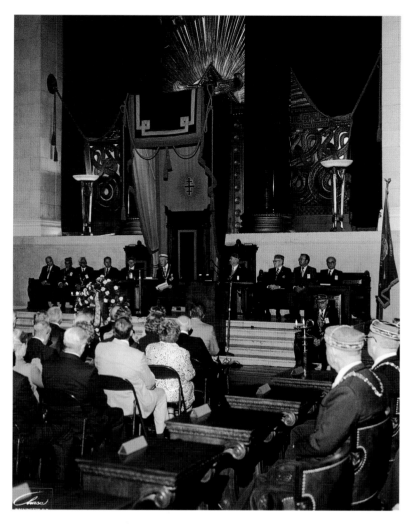

Clausen with Grand
Commander Alberto
Mansur of Brazil.

Biennial session in a
packed temple room.

Clausen being conducted
to the symbolic East
during the 1977 session
of the Supreme Council.

1985–2001

PILLARS OF CHARITY

Extending the Legacy

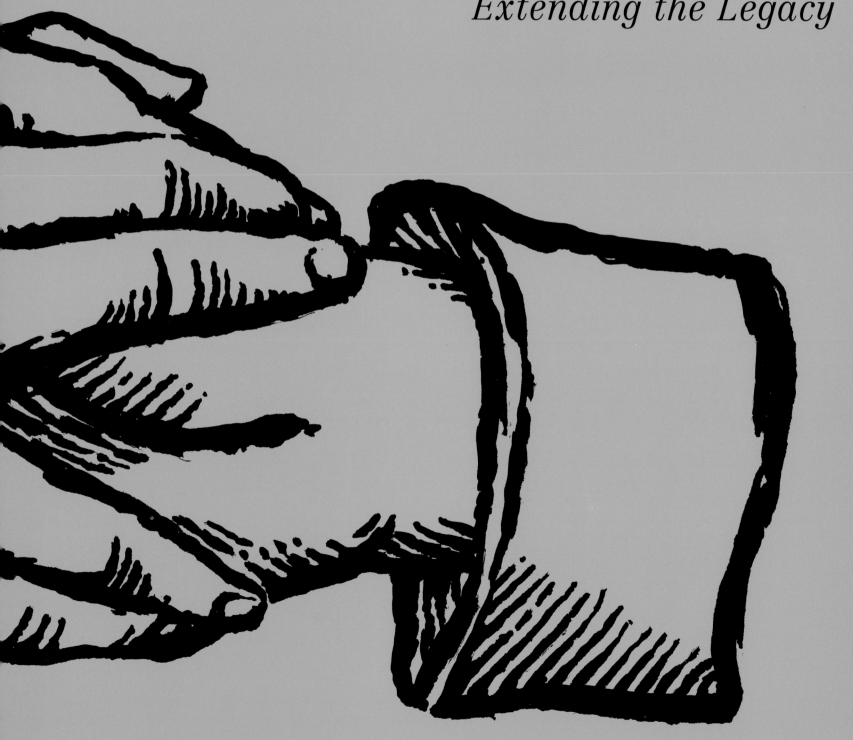

THE SCOTTISH RITE, nearly as old as the United States, is now entering its third century. Through peace and war, abundance and want, expansion and restraint, both the fraternity and the country where it had its start survive and prosper. By the time Fred Kleinknecht assumed leadership in 1985, he had served under four of the six prior Sovereign Grand Commanders in the twentieth century. No other leader in the history of the Scottish Rite could claim a compar-

244

able advantage of continuity with his predecessors. And few could claim a better understanding of the values, strengths, and motives of the institution and its membership. At the heart of American Scottish Rite Freemasonry, a powerful spirit of generosity is driven by a centuries-old tradition of meeting social need, and philanthropic programs have been an important part of activities in the Southern Jurisdiction for decades. Today, under the leadership of Grand

Commander Kleinknecht, the same spirit and tradition are served in new and creative ways. As it has done with unparalleled success for two hundred years, the fraternity combines the best parts of the past with the unprecedented resources and opportunities of the present, to carve the building blocks for its exciting future. The metaphor of the double-headed eagle, with one face toward history and the other looking ahead, has never been more timely.

Grand Commander
Christian Frederick
Kleinknecht, Jr.

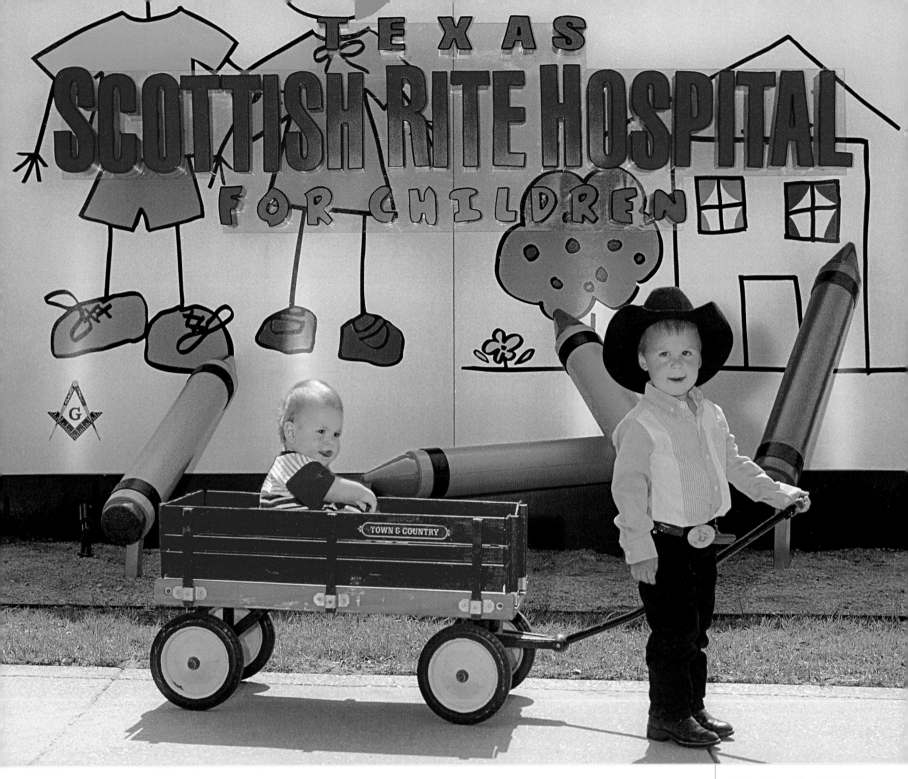

At the Texas Scottish Rite Hospital for Children in Dallas, the Masonic tradition of brother helping brother —and brothers helping others—rolls on.

Masonic philanthropies give away more than $2,000,000 every day, nearly two-thirds in support of public hospitals, and another 30 percent to maintain Masonic medical and housing facilities, such as this Scottish Rite Hospital for Children in Dallas.

Another $40 million-plus each year goes to medical research, community services, scholarships and youth activities, and Masonic museums and buildings which are open to the public.

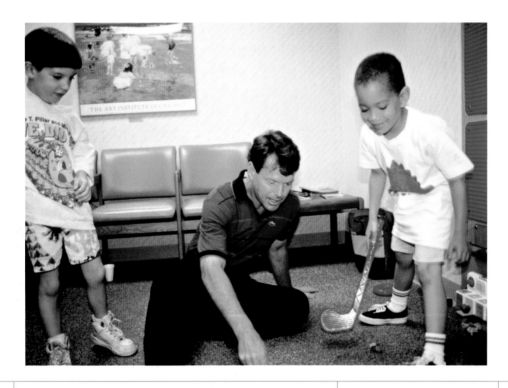

The first Scottish Rite programs for childhood language disorders began in the early 1950s. Today, the Scottish Rite maintains clinics, centers, and programs in every state of the Union, helping preschool children of all races and creeds, regardless of Masonic relationship or the family's ability to pay. In one of them, champion golfer Tom Watson checks out the putting surface on the reception room carpet for a couple of future Tiger Woods.

"Definitely one of George's thousand points of light." That's how Barbara Bush describes Masonic medical and learning programs for children. At the Texas Scottish Rite Hospital, the First Lady helps dish out the goodies to a diminutive medical staff.

Children's Healthcare of Atlanta offers a modern paradigm for the ideals set forth in these words to the African Lodge, delivered by the Right Worshipful Master Prince Hall in 1792. "I shall therefore endeavor to shew the duty of a Mason...as love and benevolence to all the family of mankind, as God's make and creation, therefore we ought to love them all, for love or hatred is of the whole kind, for if I love a man for the sake of the image of God which is on him, I must love all, for He made all, and upholds all, and we are dependent upon him for all we do enjoy and expect to enjoy in this world and that which is to come.

Therefore, he [the Mason] will help and assist all his fellow-men in distress, let them be of what colour or nation they may, yea, even our very enemies, much more a brother mason."

The Childhood Language
Center at Richmond,
Virginia is one of well
over 100 such centers,
clinics, and programs
now operating through-
out the United States.

254

Grand Commander Kleinknecht presents a fraternal ring to one-time cowboy, singer, movie star, and sports magnate Gene Autry, a Scottish Rite Mason since 1927.

Longtime Scottish Rite Mason Ernest Borgnine is enlisted by his friend and fishing companion, Fred Kleinknecht, to produce an animated video in support of Scottish Rite language-disorder programs. The Oscar-winning star's voice and reputation help make "On the Wings of Words" an instant success.

America's folksinger laureate and 33rd Degree Mason, Burl Ives is a frequent entertainer at Scottish Rite events, particularly in support of the growing Masonic charities.

The first and only honorary membership in the Scottish Rite is presented to President Ronald Reagan at the White House by Shriner Imperial Potentate Voris King, Grand Commander (NMJ) Francis Paul, and Grand Commander Kleinknecht.

President George Bush accepts a drawing of himself and First Lady Barbara Bush with their grandchildren, presented by Grand Commander Kleinknecht in gratitude for their support of the Scottish Rite's Childhood Language Disorder Center in Washington, D.C.

256 Dean of New York's Marble Collegiate Church and America's leading inspirational writer of the twentieth century, Norman Vincent Peale was an ardent Blue Lodge and Scottish Rite Freemason. (In 1952 his book *The Power of Positive Thinking* outsold everything but the Bible.)

A frequent chaplain at biennial meetings of the Supreme Council, in 1993, the year before his death, Peale authored an article for the *Scottish Rite Journal* defending the complementary relationship between the fraternity and organized religion.

The Dynamics of Freedom, a book on American values published by the Scottish Rite, is presented to Chief Justice of the United States Warren Berger.

In parallel with the Scottish Rite's new philanthropic outreach, there is a turning inward as well to the rediscovery—and demythologizing—of ancient Masonic tradition. Woven together, the dual strands of charity and heritage define the new fabric of fraternity.

The 200th anniversary of the laying of the cornerstone of the Capitol of the United States is celebrated on September 18, 1993, with ceremonies rededicating this "Temple of Democracy." Grand Commander Kleinknecht addresses the huge crowd, and then an officer of the lodge consecrates the cornerstone with an offering of wine, corn, and oil and uses his working tools to confirm that the stone is square, level, and true.

The Capitol cornerstone used in the reenactment ceremonies is received into the collection of the Scottish Rite, Southern Jurisdiction. Accepting it are: George R. Adams, Grand Master, Free and Accepted Masons of the District of Columbia; Nathaniel Adams, Jr., his counterpart in the Prince Hall Affiliation,

District of Columbia; Grand Commander Kleinknecht; Claude H. Harris III, Master of Alexandria-Washington Lodge No. 22; and Col. Frank W. Harris, National President of National Sojourners, Inc.

In the Robert Burns Room of the House of the Temple, Stephen Joel Trachtenberg (center), a 33rd Degree Mason and president of The George Washington University, watches as C. Fred Kleinknecht greets Susan Phillips, Dean of GW's School of Business and Public Management, at a book signing for Trachetenberg's *Thinking Out Loud.*

Working in close collaboration, Trachtenberg and Kleinknecht revitalized a longtime educational partnership between GW and the Scottish Rite.

Facing the future, this delegation from the Supreme Council of the Ivory Coast assembles at the House of the Temple for the last biennial session of the twentieth century.

Once more creating order out of chaos, Grand Commander Kleinknecht set about restoring and refurbishing the House of the Temple, in serious disrepair after decades of deferred restoration. No doubt both Pike and Cowles would have approved, not only for the dramatic results of the ambitious project, but for its method, honoring the past in a way that defines and supports a leader's vision of the future of the fraternity.

Definitely not your father's Freemason, actor-comedian Michael Richards is a Knight Commander of the Court of Honour of the Scottish Rite. Known to millions as the quirky, hilarious "hipster-doofus," Cosmo Kramer, Richards contributed much to the historic success of television's "Seinfeld." He brings the same energy and commitment to his support of numerous Scottish Rite charities, inspired by his mentor, the late Red Skelton, also a Scottish Rite Mason.

One such charity is the Scottish Rite Childhood Language Disorders Clinics. At the Supreme Council biennial gala banquet in October 1999, Richards leads the applause, with Grand Commander Kleinknecht, master-of-ceremonies Stephen Joel Trachtenberg, and Dr. Tommie L. Robinson, Director of the Washington, D.C., clinic, at an emotional high point in the evening's program. Several months before, when Briana Mendez first came to the clinic, she was unable to speak without stuttering. "As you can see, I feel good when I talk now," she told her rapt audience. "I love going to the Scottish Rite Center.... I would like to thank them for helping me."

Thanks indeed.

Grand Commander Kleinknecht received delegates from the Prince Hall Scottish Rite Supreme Councils at the House of the Temple on April 18, 2001. His presentation of the *Revised Standard Pike Ritual* to Grand Commanders Samuel Bragdon Jr. and Edgar Bridges continued an amicable tradition begun by Albert Pike who shared the Scottish Rite rituals with the Prince Hall leadership in the 1880s. Once again, the past is prologue.

This Supreme Council, convened for the biennial meeting in 1999, will preside into the new millennium and see the Scottish Rite into the start of its third century.

Alexandria–Washington Lodge No. 22, A.F.&A.M., Alexandria, Virginia, 155 (lower)

The American Academy of Arts and Letters, New York, 139 (lower left)

The Chancellor Robert R. Livingston Masonic Library of Grand Lodge, New York, 31, 33 (upper), 36 (upper left), 39 (upper), 62 (right), 68, 73 (middle), 76, 121 (lower left), 164, 165 (lower)

Childhood Language Center, Richmond, Virginia, 252, 253

Arturo de Hoyos, 8, 18 (upper), 22, 23, 24, 25, 29 (left), 44, 80, 89 (lower right), 160 (upper left, lower left), 168, 242

Mark A. Fastoso, 96, 104, 180

William Geiger, 260, 264

The George Washington National Masonic Memorial Library, Alexandria, Virginia, 190, 191, 216

The George Washington University, Washington, D.C., 259

Grand Orient of France, Library and Archives, Paris, 21

Holak Collection of the Performing Arts Archives of the University of Minnesota Libraries, Minneapolis, 178 (upper), 179

Leo Baeck Institute, New York, New York, 206 (lower)

Library of Congress, Washington, D.C., 20 (upper), 54 (right), 66, 69, 78, 115, 120, 132, 134 (right), 144 (right), 154, 158, 163, 175 (lower), 181, 186 (upper), 187, 211

Earl MacDonald, 257, 258, 263

Maxwell Mackenzie, 259, 270

National Museum of American History, Smithsonian Institution, Washington, D.C., 27 (lower)

Performing Arts Archives of the University of Minnesota Libraries, Minneapolis, 178 (lower)

Pierson Photography, Falls Church, Virginia, 27 (upper right), 155 (upper left & right)

Potomac Lodge No. 5, F.A.A.M., Washington, D.C., 39 (lower)

H. Wallace Reid, 53 (upper)

Reunion des Museum Nationaux, Chateau Versailles et de Trianon, photo © RMN, 27 (upper left)

Tony Rodriguez, Classic Professional Photography, Bowie, Maryland, 261

The Schomburg Center for Research in Black Culture, Photographs and Prints Division, New York Public Library, Astor, Lenox and Tilden Foundations, New York, 105

Scottish Rite Hospital for Children, Atlanta, Georgia, 249, 251

The South Carolina Historical Society, Charleston, South Carolina, 51

The Supreme Council of the Netherlands in The Hague, Evert Kwaadgras, Curator to the Grand East of the Netherlands, 56 – 57

Texas Scottish Rite Hospital for Children, 248, 250 (upper)

John Trumbull, *The Death of General Warren at the Battle of Bunker Hill, 17 June 1775* Yale University Art Gallery, Trumbull Collection, 40

United States Holocaust Memorial Museum, Washington, D.C., 206 (upper)

Valley of Albany, New York, and Supreme Council, A.A.S.R., Northern Masonic Jurisdiction, Photograph by David Bohl, 26 (upper)

All other materials reproduced in this book are the property of The Supreme Council, 33°, Southern Jurisdiction, Archives, Library, and Museum, Washington, D.C. Principal photography by Lee B. Ewing.

Page references in roman type indicate text. Page references in italic type indicate illustrations.

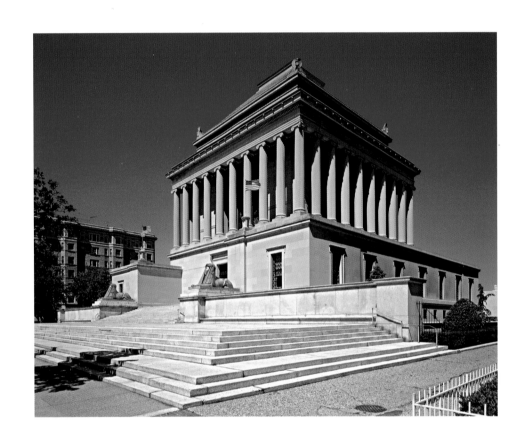